JOHN BYE

YOU WONT GET THE HUMP WHEN YOU EAT MY RUMP

Life As A London Butcher

THE DEBUT NOVEL FROM THE AUTHOR THAT'S SPENT NEARLY 4 DECADES IN THE MEAT GAME AND LEARNED THE ART OF SELLING TO THOUSANDS OF LONDONERS OVER THAT TIME. MEETING THAT MANY PEOPLE, YOU'RE GOING TO HAVE PLENTY OF STORIES TO TELL... SOME WILL MAKE YOU LAUGH AND OTHERS WILL REALLY MOVE YOU.

An honest account of life growing up in a working class family in London and discovering the hard way to be the best you can

I really enjoyed this book, filled with humor and tragedy. Great to know what goes on behind the counter.

Terry Battenbough

A book of personal stories touching on family, personal and working relationships while doing what you can to make it through the emotional minefield without losing your head.

.

Preface

This book is a brief summary of my life growing up in North East London and the reason why I became a Butcher.

From my early childhood I lived in a number of different places called "home" growing up as my father looked constantly for the big pay day. From a toddler until the age of seven, we lived in New Southgate, but our family eventually settled down in Enfield, a borough of London and this is where my life in butchery began.

First, I followed the footsteps of my dad, John senior and later making my own path. I'll take you on trip around the suburban areas of the capital city from 1979 for a decade, mainly in North London, sprinkled with some action in East and West of the Metropolis followed by a short diversion up the M1 into Bedfordshire and Northamptonshire for a couple of years until London came calling again in 1990. I will tell you about the fights with other staff and customers when things got out of hand.

In this book you will learn the idiosyncratic butcher language, back slang or kcab gnals as we know it plus find out what went on behind the counter when we wasn't cutting meat or serving customers. At the end of the book, I have written up to date insider tips on the best time to visit your local independent butcher or supermarket chain so you can avoid getting sold the crap cuts but instead have a tender, tasty piece of meat on your dinner plate.

Oh, the title, yes I nearly forgot to mention, "You won't get the hump when you eat my rump" was one of many cheeky calls that butchers would use in market-style shops and stalls to cause a commotion or get a reaction from passers-by, hopefully with them ending up buying some meat!

Are you ready for the journey?

I hope you enjoy my story and up to date guides for the inside knowledge to butchery. If you are interested in knowing more about other books that I'm writing or what I've covered in this book, please contact me at johnbyeauthor@gmail.com or follow me on facebook/johnbyeauthor

John

CONTENTS OF BOOK

FOR MY DAD, JOHN BYE.

CHAPTER 1
And So It Begins

I don't remember much about my early life apart from the rather odd memory of being in the back seat of an old Ford popular 100E around 1969 listening to what I later discovered was "Something Happening" by Herman's Hermits when I was four years old. I was being driven by a family member on my dad's side to someone's party in Hornsey, North London. My early memories seem to be in black and white, like the photos taken and placed in our family albums.

Mum and dad were quite young when I was born in 1965 at Bearsted memorial hospital, a Jewish community hospital in Stoke Newington. Mum nineteen, dad was twenty. Mum had been sent to London at the age of sixteen to get a job and help to provide for her ten brothers and sisters living back in Redcar, North Yorkshire. She was the third eldest of six girls and four boys. Her dad Jim was working for ICI chemical plant that produced among other things, lots of paint, in Heston which was a few miles from the family home. Her mum, Elsie, was obviously busy looking after the kids. My Dad grew up with two sisters, Pam and Shirley, in a small terrace house in Palmers Green with his mum, Winifred and dad, Arthur. Mum got a job in Golders green, North London as a nanny to a Jewish family's two children and dad was working at this time for the footballers, Jimmy Greaves and his Tottenham Hotspur teammate, Cliff Jones, who had opened up their own butcher shop It lasted for a few months before he left and went to work for a Jewish butcher called "Franks", also in Arnos Grove, North London. To cut a long story short, the two of them met in a pub in 1964, called "The Cambridge Arms" that is now gone and been replaced by a roundabout on the A10 trunk road. Mum got pregnant so they got married in January 1965, and I came along in June, the same year. My early years were spent with mum and dad up and down England as dad chased the jobs paying the best wages. We lived in a little tied cottage close to Keswick, Cumbria, as dad got a job as a lumberjack for the forestry commission but my mum hated the isolation so, we moved to Redcar, close to the seafront and many arcades that entertained the holidaymakers that filled this once busy fishing village but was now the home to the nationalised British Steel and multinational conglomerate ICI chemical plant. These companies were the financial lifeline of the whole region, so dad got a job with British steel, thanks to my uncle Tony who was a union rep and had much influence at this time. We stayed for a few months before returning to London, getting a brand new council flat in New Southgate, North East London, in the spring of 1967.

In September 1967, I was joined by my brother Mark, who was born in North Middlesex Hospital. Me and Mark had a great relationship as according to my mum I only tried to kill him once when he was about two years old when I tried to suffocate by putting a sofa cushion on his face but came in the nick of time to stop me from taking out her baby! During 1969 at the age of four and a bit, I had my first encounter of a butcher shop. Dad became the manager of a shop called "Bunkers" (named after the owner who lived upstairs with his nine kids!). I was bought in for a couple of hours in the summer when it was quiet and watched with interest when dad would be serving the customers coming in and I would be introduced as his boy. I would be given a sixpence which is two and a half pence in old money, before the United Kingdom went decimalised in nineteen seventy one, by a nice old lady and rushed off to the paper shop to get my favourite bottle of Tizer fizzy drink and once quickly drunk I would return the empty bottle and claim my old one penny deposit. There was an extra interest as a garage next door built saloon cars for track racing and my dad would take me to meet the mechanics and their cars. This is where my love of fast cars began, as I would buy or get to drive many sports cars over the years.

In the days where the home phone could be on a shared line and one would pick up the phone and hear someone else talking, we received a call of another kind in October 1972, when police officers called at our second floor flat to inform dad that his dad, Arthur, had died at the age of fifty one having a single massive heart attack. It was the first time I had seen dad cry and it made me cry too seeing him obviously devastated. This was the first loss of a member of my family that I had encountered and I remember the grief shown by everyone at his funeral when he was cremated at a cemetery in Aldershot. I had last seen my granddad with my nan in June 1972 when me and my brother were being taken for a short holiday down to Basingstoke where my grandparents had recently moved to and while driving along the A30, witnessed the devastating British European Airways Flight 548 crash, which took the lives of all 118 passengers on board. There was carnage and chaos everywhere, as fire fighters and policemen and women were taking control of the scene. I remember the big Green outside broadcast vans of the BBC lined along the side of the carriageway and travelling vehicles just stopped and people got out and look at the wreckage. My Granddad went to look while me, Mark and Nan looked on. Rather than heading to my grandparents' house, we were taken to dad's sister, Pam, where we watched on the television what we had witnessed for ourselves, earlier in real life.

CHAPTER 2
Changes Afoot

In December 1972, our sister, Samantha, was born and then from that moment on the world and pecking order changed for the Bye brothers when our little sister arrived. She was treat like a little toy, with both me and Mark wanting to push her around in her buggy in the street where we lived so we could show her off to our neighbours after we finished school. I don't think mum objected as she always said it was ok and she appreciated the break from us being under her feet, especially two young noisy boys who frequently got into scrapes. One afternoon it went very wrong most notably, when me, Mark and two other brothers who lived in the bottom of Betspath House decided to jump from the building adjacent to our block of flats that housed the big wheelie dustbin and sheds that stood around three meters high. We would climb up the rails that jutted out from the brick walls, finding anything to hang on to until we reached the roof as if we were making the ascent to the top of a mountain where we would survey all below us. We took all took turns hanging from the roof and then letting go, falling to the concrete path below us. I decided to go first, scurrying feet on the brick wall, trying to hold on with my toes, fingers tightly gripped to the ledge, waiting for the perfect moment to let go. And then I did. My feet hit the ground, stinging as they hit the concrete, falling back on to my arse, but none the worse for my unstylish landing. The two brothers followed suit and jumped, landed without a problem. My brother followed up at the rear and though he was small and his nickname was skinny because of his small frame, he had no fear. He let go and somehow managed to turn one hundred and eighty degrees, crashing on to his left arm and head. I fucking shit myself as for a brief time he didn't move. He started screaming with pain so I left him with the cook brothers, running the two flights of stairs to let mum know and get her to call for an ambulance. When the paramedics arrived, they moved quickly to get mark comfortable, before rushing him off to North Middlesex hospital. Scans showed he had fractured his skull and broke his arm which was quite scary as he was only five. Mark stayed in hospital for two weeks, coming home to be cared for by mum and with help from her sister Chrissy, looking after Samantha when skinny need some attention. While my brother was recovering from his injuries, our primary school, Garfield, was being closed down to make way for a new housing development and the new replacement was literally the other side of the road from our flat. What a result for me as I wouldn't have to drag my little brother to school half a mile away to the old building anymore! When Mark was allowed to play outside when his cast came off, I took him to the local sweetshop that was run by a couple who would occasionally leave the shop empty while they nipped out to the back room to put the kettle on. I placed my brother on the front door, holding it open and also look out, while I crept in, filled my pockets with sweets and chewing gum, legging it out of the shop, both of us running as fast as we could to a little hideout in a building site to share our stolen booty.

One of the few times that dad lost his temper and got

physical with me was when one afternoon he had been taking our dog Sheba, a large German Shepard, for a walk and was evidently pissed off doing this which manifested when he opened the front door of our home, us three kids were playing in the hallway with my baby sister sitting upright watching as me and Mark played. The dog came bounding in full of energy and ran straight over Samantha, bowling her over and knocking her head on the hard floor. She screamed and wailed loudly, this making dad see red, grabbed me by my tee shirt with one hand , threw me violently across my bedroom like a rag doll , only the wall stopping my flight as my feet never touched the ground. I was petrified, not coming out of my room for the rest of the day. We would shortly be on the move from New Southgate. In the summer of 1974, when we moved to Waltham Gardens, a former garden nursery used by Italian prisoners of war, after the second world war, that was pulled down by the borough council, replacing the glasshouses with fifty houses and flats for families from around Enfield and Haringey. Our new home seemed like the countryside at the time to me, with its many undeveloped green areas around us. Me, my brother and sister loved growing up in Waltham Gardens, a newly built council estate where other young families had moved to. Two brothers, Darren and Des, joined up with me and Mark, to go thieving from the maisonettes that were still being built in Waltham Gardens. We "borrowed" enough materials to build our own Go Cart. The chassis, seat and steering were bits of broken scaffold boards, the wheels from an old pram .We painted it up in the blue paint used in the kitchens of the new flats and called our set of wheels," Cockney Rebel", after Steve Harley's band of the same name

During 1975 dad partnered up with a business associate called Brian Thomas, who was the money man and dad the technician and they bought two shops in North London. One was trading as Rawles in Green Lanes, Haringey and the other that I don't remember the name, was in Firs Lane, Palmers green. The shop in Firs Lane was named "J. A. Bye family butchers" after dad and was my next step into my destiny in the meat game. In 1976 I worked during the summer holidays, cooking fat to make dripping. This was also the time when I first went to Smithfield market as it was, pre glass walled cutting areas and food safety systems that are part and parcel of the modern Smithfield market today, through Hazard Analysis and Critical Control Point or HACCP. This is enforced by the food standards agency, in the wake of BSE and foot and mouth outbreaks in the nineteen nineties and two thousands. Up until this point, the shops were open and you could walk through from one shop to another, dodging hanging sides of beef, lambs and pigs. All my senses were being ambushed by what was going on around me. I was fascinated by loud noisy shopmen, taking the piss out of work colleagues, selling carcasses and boxed meat. The smell of fresh cut livestock was everywhere and it was an aroma that I came to love, especially when I had been on annual leave from my place of work in later years, filling my nose with the smell of steaks and sawdust! Smithfield Market was run by the transport and general workers union at this time and you couldn't move any meat from the shop you bought from, without using a Porter or Bummeree who would collect your meat and bring it to your vehicle. Incidentally, the late Queen Mother was an honorary Bummeree. The market would start trading at midnight and usually be closed by 11am. There was a pub called "The Cock" that was open at the same time situated within the market, where you would find a few "dodgy" deals being hatched, late night revellers and alcoholic workers in the early hours. Dad's meat mover was an ex professional boxer called Tommy McGovern who fought in the 1950's and still looked tough. I always remember how smart he looked with his trimmed goatee beard as he pulled his barrow about loaded with various cuts. In 1978, dad split with his business partner, probably over money and decided to leave the meat trade. He next went on to his craziest job he'd ever taken on by becoming a rag & bone man; collecting scrap from homes and businesses and selling it on, riding on a trap pulled along by a horse with a gentleman by the name of "Bob The Totter". This lasted for a few months until he found a job advertised for a butcher (Matthews) in Enfield Town. It was a time when money was tight at home, the electricity was cut off more than once and dad had to borrow a generator to power a few lights and an Electric heater. Thankfully it was for only a few days until he got paid and sorted out the outstanding bills. I was twelve years old and mum had decided that I had to get a job, as me and Mark were always scrapping. I'd found a paper round job, delivering the daily papers to local residents, where I was paid the princely sum of £4 per week for 5 hours a week. I received an extra £1 for helping sort the newspapers into different routes for delivery. After several months at Matthews, dad got promoted to store manager; that was THE opportunity for me to start as a daily after school cleaner. I was addressed as the yob because as you will discover, butchers have their own slang language, where you talk, saying words backwards (roughly), hence I was the *"YOB"* or boy. I was given a tough time by dad who didn't want to be seen or heard giving me an easy time in front of the rest of the guys. I got all the shit jobs as is required of the *yob* but with an extra slap or kick if I complained. After a couple of months, my resistance had worn off and now I was treated with a touch more respect. 1979 was the end of tough times in the UK, as many people were unemployed so when Margaret Thatcher came to power, there was a change in mood felt by everyone, some optimistic that things would get better, more jobs, more money. The shop seemed like it had a revolving door, with staff changing monthly as experienced butchers looked for an extra tenner in their pay packet. Salaries at the time were comparatively low, with an average salary for a butcher approximately £110 per week before stoppages. We had a core group who stayed at the shop unless they got promoted and rewarded with their own shop to manage. Dad was the manager or *REGANAM*, Alfie or *ESON* because of his large nose, 2nd in command, Nicky, the chief cutter, big Dave, little Dave, sniffer Brian and Doug. We had two ladies who were the main sales assistants, Linda and Anne.

CHAPTER 3
Showtime

Anne and Linda were supported by two to three part time staff depending on the time of year, like Christmas, where we staffed up. There was always a lot of sexual banter going on between the cashiers and senior management who ran the shops who would come in from time to time to chat up their favourite girls. There was always gossip about who was fucking who. By the time I was fourteen I was working on a Saturday as well as after school five days per week. I would have to go with dad on Saturdays so this meant getting up at 4.30am to get in for 5.30am start. As time went on I was watching and asking the butchers about what they were doing and Nicky, the chief cutter in particular, would explain in detail what he was boning out or slicing and let me have a go, under supervision. I would start asking for more things to do and I knew it would save the butchers' time if I could pick up a few skills. I started with lamb fores or shorts as they are called that are the animals' front two shoulders and neck. As Matthews was owned by Borthwick, we could buy lots of New Zealand lamb subsidised by our parent company and so we would have up to three hundred lambs per week to cut up into joints. I would separate the shoulder from neck, using a boning knife to cut the meat clean from the ribs attached to the neck. Within weeks, I was cutting out fifty shorts per week, ten per evening after school and placing the prepared cuts in the mutton cloth that protects the lamb during its long shipment and then storing them in the freezer until they were needed. I was beginning to become an asset though I didn't realise it at the time. I guess my dad who told me to call him "boss" or "reg" short for *reganam*, manager backwards (yeah, I know, complicated!) and never dad, had told the lads to start training me without my knowledge. I was still washing up the trays and the greens that go in between the trays plus clean the bogs and the kitchen/office. If I was lucky, Nicky would ask me to walk with him to do the daily banking at the post office. I looked up to Nick like he was my big brother. He came from a big Irish family and was the youngest of several siblings so he treated me tough in the shop but was always giving advice about girls and work. He was nineteen and a heavy smoker and drinker, but a good looking charmer, never short of a bird that he would tell me he was shagging. I lost contact with him in subsequent years. He would later came to my wedding to Debbie, along with his girlfriend, Jeanette, who I went to comprehensive school with. She was a year older than me and was a crazy fucker who at the time was a skinhead and fought like a boy hard as nails. After we left school, we ended up being friends, I was sixteen and she was seventeen; we would drink regularly in a pub called Prince Albert, in Enfield highway. Anyway, back to my wedding night; Nick turned up with Jeanette and we spoke about our small world and how I knew his girlfriend. I saw Nick once more after that, driving a bus and again a couple of years later, driving a Pickford's removals lorry. I'd learnt much later in the early 2000's, he died from lung cancer at the age of fourty nine.

By 1980 at the age of fifteen, I was starting to cut whole lambs and the opportunity was always there due to the amount we had in stock. It was in this year that we had a great deal of publicity, though the company didn't capitalise on the situation as my dad did. Enfield Town had been picked by our parent company, Borthwick, to host a documentary team from TV channel 1 from New Zealand, who were making a programme about how the UK was receiving whole New Zealand lambs and selling them cheaper than back in their native home. The day before the TV unit arrived there was Nicky, little Dave and myself cutting up a hundred lambs as quickly as possible, ready for the big event. Dad let me miss school and I went in with him at 4.30am on a Wednesday morning. All the other lads turned up shortly after and we put on a massive lamb show. The float in the shop window (four steel tubes hanging on chains from the ceiling) had fourty shoulders and fourty legs hanging identically, with all the price tickets in a straight line with plastic flat leaf parsley on. The rails over the serve, over the counter and back wall were also covered in lamb joints

Chapter 4
Early Starts

The show was on around 8.30am and we waited in anticipation for the local paper, "The Enfield Advertiser" and the butchers trade paper, "Meat Trades Journal", to arrive as they had been informed of the arrival of the film crew. It was funny as dad and Alfie posed in various parts of the shop in front of the lamb hanging from the rails. Around lunchtime, the TV crew arrived and the producer of the show spoke to my dad and advised him what he would like to do without too much disruption to the running of the shop. . The single cameraman and sound man spoke to the presenter of the show, got set and then started filming. The lads took the piss when I was approached by the cameraman and asked if I would cut up a lamb and be filmed but I declined as I didn't want to fuck it up as I didn't have much confidence at the time, being a fifteen year old going through puberty!

I was also serving the customers coming into the shop on Saturdays which was my day off school, using the old style NCR piano cash register, still with the half pence on it! This was a great experience, giving me a massive amount of confidence, interacting with hundreds of people per day plus flirting with Teresa, the sixteen year old Saturday girl who was a year older than me and was a very sexy teenager. She teased me and the other young butchers, using her sexuality to get her way. She and little Dave would have sex in the girl's toilets. We were all horny fuckers and I would have my fair share of dates with various Saturday girls but not mature enough to have sex with them.

About 12 months of learning in my after school time, dad could see I was destined to become a trainee after leaving school and started to turn a blind eye if I bunked school and turned up at the shop earlier than I should have. I asked him if I could open the shop on a Saturday morning and get all the return float above the serve over counter filled with lamb joints. He agreed so I got up on the first Saturday at 4.00am and cycled the four miles to Enfield Town, so excited and nervous. I was determined to get the show on as quickly as possible, taking out thirty lamb shorts, and weighing and hanging sixty shoulders of lamb. The same was done with the legs of lamb, I was very pleased with myself as the butchers started to come in and see the show was on. Looking back, I was just hungry to learn, I didn't care how much shit I took mentally or physically.

During spring 1980, dad told me to take the day off school; so I was going to look at a shop with him and the district manager, Ron. I didn't say anything, I just listened. Ron drove us to Canning Town, East London. We had stopped by Rathbone Market, a busy shopping area, in particular to look at an empty butchers shop that Ron had spotted while working in the Matthews shop in the area. I listened with excitement as Ron, who I idolised as he was only twenty four at the time and had been promoted to district manager, taking overall charge of fifteen shops, told me that he and dad would be buying the shop and I would be working in there, on my own initially, then if it took off, they would join me. I continued my usual routine of getting through school and rushing out at 3.15pm,

Monday to Friday, catch the 217 or 310 to Enfield Town. About a month later, dad told me to miss school for the week as he had got a stall on Edmonton Green market and I was to work in it. Unfortunately, it was shit trade wise, so we pulled out after a couple of days. The good thing was he said I could work in the shop for the rest of the week but disappear if our current area manager, Tom, should make a visit. Tom was a man who was in his late fifties, very much respected by the shop staff.

Being physically assaulted was a normal occurrence for the younger members of staff and as I was quite small, I tended to get more than my fair share of punches to the body and even got bitten! I'm not sure if was just the normal rite of passage endured by the many lads working up and down the country, but it sure happened a lot in our shop.

CHAPTER 5
End Of School

Tom was a man who had earned his reputation as a butcher of experience though I never saw him cut anything, it was just the way dad talked about him with respect. Tom was always polite and greeted me whenever he visited the shop. He gave me a piece of advice as a yob that has stayed with me for nearly four decades when one late afternoon visit, he approached me and said "cleanliness is next to godliness". Not earth shattering I know but a good piece of advice nonetheless. At school, I was in my final year at Bullsmoor secondary school, though my education there was shrinking due to bunking lessons and going to work earlier in the days. Me and my friend Des, who lived a couple of doors away, would meet up at the bottom of Waltham Gardens where we lived and either head for Waltham Cross to walk around the local shopping precinct, looking in the clothes shops and record stores, or visit his older brothers girlfriend, Yvonne. She was around nineteen and out of work at the time, so was happy to take us in for a couple of hours. We would talk about usual teenage angst while listening to her music, like McFadden and Whitehead, Shalamar, Lips Inc., artists that were in the charts at the time. This was when I started smoking and trying to establish an identity for myself, listening to music and being influenced by the pop stars of the late 1970's and the start of the new decade. Christmas 1980, I'd received a Realistic record turntable as a Christmas present from mum & dad and with money I'd saved in my abbey national savings account, I bought my first couple of seven inch singles, Pink Floyd's "Another brick in the wall" which was the big hit of 1979/1980, plus a single by ex Ultravox singer, John Foxx, called "Underpass". I was good at sports, playing for the school football team, but my strengths lie in athletics. I never had the motivation to train much though I did consider applying to join Enfield Harriers, though my lack of confidence held me back. I ran for the school at 800m and 1500m track events where I had stamina to always be in the top three but I enjoyed cross country running the most. I'd bought myself Adidas spikes as I got more serious, running in inter-school competitions, then being picked by the Borough of Enfield to run in a London borough competition. My proudest moment without doubt, was when Mister Barrand, our sports teacher, called in to one of my classes and pulled me out to talk to me. I thought I was in for a bollocking as I was becoming a pain in the arse, fucking around in lesson or bunking off school. He informed me that I had been picked to run for Middlesex in the South of England County championship held at Hillingdon. I remember it was bloody freezing as there were literally hundreds of school boys trying to get a good start, jostling at the start line. I hadn't trained for at least three weeks but I gave all I had and finished sixty fourth. To add to my disappointment, my big toenail went black and fell off a week later. That was the end of my running days. In March 1980, I was told to report to the careers officer, who spoke to me when I sat down, asking what I'd like to do when I left school. I told him I was working in the shop but I did enjoy technical drawing, which was one of my lessons. There was a school work scheme called trident and a local engineering company called E and E Kaye were offering a placement for the three weeks of the scheme. To my disappointment, I didn't get an opportunity but there was a garage with an opportunity to work with cars that was my other passion so I grabbed it, anything to get off school. I turned up to work the following week but I only lasted a few days. I didn't get on with the main mechanic so I just decided there and then to get to Enfield and be with the lads in the shop. I left school in May 1981. I remember the feeling of relief as I rushed out the school building and seeing my fellow students writing on friends and other pupils clothes, signing their names or throwing flour and eggs at each other. I sprinted to the bus stop, never looking back.

CHAPTER 6
Back To School Again

I had to go back at the end of May and start of June 1981 to complete my exams. I'd taken the obligatory English and maths, along with French, Technical Drawing, Art and Metalwork, which I failed miserably at every one of them, but I didn't care. I had left school and had been working in Matthews, Enfield, full time for a few weeks. Nicky started showing me to break down Topbits (rear leg) and Forequarter (shoulder) of beef. We cut more ponies, no, not horse meat but the trade term for the ribs and the best parts of the shoulder muscles. Dad told me I was to go to Matthews training college, based at the headquarters in St. John's Street, close to Smithfield market. I was to be trained in basic cutting skills plus book keeping skills which included how to work profit percentage on the various cuts of beef, lamb and pork carcase. The class was made up of several school leavers, who were yobs in shops from different areas of the south of England. I had worked with two of the lads, Barry, who I would work with in Harlow terminus for the following summer months as part of my on -going training and also Steve, a 17 year old who I would end up working with for nearly a year in our Camden high Street shop. I was confident, bordering on cocky as all the lads in Enfield said I would piss the course and I did have a lot of knowledge for a sixteen year old, so I was full of myself. The course was run by Barry and Tim who were both butchers by trade but for health reasons, couldn't work in the shop. Barry had a heart pacemaker fitted that I remembered was affected by certain frequencies or something like that and at times didn't work properly so he would be feeling and looking shit, so then the class would be run by Tim, who was affectionately known as peg leg as he had stabbed himself in the groin while cutting lambs I think and lost a lot of blood as he'd severed his femoral artery. He ended up losing his leg and Matthews didn't have a leg (pun intended) to stand on legally as we should be wearing stab pads as per operating systems manual and no one was made to wear them, so they got Tim a nice payoff, a company car and the cushy training job. I was also learning my trade at Harlow, with Duncan who I had worked with at Enfield Town when I was still at school and he was dad's first hand, before Alfie, got promoted to store manager, with Harlow his first management position. (35 years later, I'm working with him again!) It was great fun working with him as I didn't have the same pressure on me as I got when working at fifty eight shop. There was a great team, with the butchers working downstairs in cutting room. Steve, Keith and trainee butcher, Barry who I was on the college training course with at Smithfield. On the shop floor, was Duncan, Albert, plus the two cashiers, Debbie and Angela. Duncan lived near Enfield Town so would drop me off on the Hertford road close to my home on the days I worked with him. After three months, my time of training at the college and in Harlow had finished. We were marked and ranked one to ten in line with our scores and I finished third. I can remember feeling disappointed but it was a good lesson in not being too cocky in the future.

I had learnt to cut pigs and gained more experience

during my time at the college in Smithfield and in the Harlow branch working on Topbits and Forequarters of beef. To explain about topbits and fores, when heifers (female) and steers (male) are slaughtered, they are dressed for the wholesaler, which means that the carcase is opened up to remove the interior ,the hide and head removed and then they are split down the middle into two sides ,because of the sheer size and weight of the animal. Each side is then cut into either two or three pieces. The front end or forequarter which is the shoulder is removed from the loin, normally between the tenth and eleventh rib. You are left with the hindquarter, which is the rump and loin attached to the back leg or topbit. The topbit is separated at the rump and that's left on the loin. All the slower cooking meats such as shin or stewing steak and the braising steak comes from the shoulder of the cow. Braising steaks such as the chuck, which comes from the back of the shoulder and the blade have gained popularity with their use by the celebrity chefs. Chuck is used to make fantastic burgers once it's minced, due to the higher fat content. From the scapula, you get the bola, or also known as the Jewish fillet because Jewish meat eaters don't eat anything from the rear of the cow, where the real fillet comes from, while the opposing muscle, the blade, is also known as the flat iron steak, due to the muscle flattening out as it attaches to the bone. The taste of these steaks are wonderfully rich, you can literally taste the iron in them! The ribs from the shoulder are amazing too, with the back rib as a rolled joint, top rib which is seam cut from the muscle and what has different commercial names but you may know it as the short rib.

Finally, the king of ribs, the fore or primal rib. I always have a fore rib for my Christmas beef roast and this cut is where you get your rib eye steak too, when it's boned out. And let's not forget the brisket either, which has gained massive demand due to guys and girls buying meat smokers. I love the forequarter because the variety of choice it offers plus it's great value in price, compared to the rest of the animal. Next, we have the rump and loin, which packs all the high value steaks that you buy from your butcher or restaurant, when eating out. I was taught to bone the three ribs on the loin if it was to be divided for sirloin, so I cut the loin where the fillet tail begins. The rest of the loin is used for t bone steaks, sirloin on one side of the bone, fillet, the other side. If you are a greedy bastard, get the butcher to cut a 600g steak, you will be very happy! Finally, the topbit. This is where all the boneless beef joints are cut from, though in recent years as the population changed, demand for roasts dwindled plus the family unit has generally gotten smaller, the butcher has adapted in the main and the three large rear leg muscles are used for steaks What we have is the thick flank, silverside and topside. To help you build a mental picture of the layout of these cuts, the thick flank is the hamstring, silverside is the outer leg muscle, topside, the inner leg muscle.

CHAPTER 7
Fights, Knockouts And The Falkland's War

The next weeks and months flew by and by early 1982, Linda and Anne had left and soon replaced by a new influx of cashiers, including a beautiful young 17 year old called Ginny who I would date and we would be together for next twelve months or so. Another of the new girls, June, was a local in her early twenties, who would get lots of visitors from friends and her boyfriend during working hours. This pissed off my dad and Alfie, who would moan about the situation. It climaxed one Saturday evening, which turned out to be June's last day. Dad had just finished the weekend knockout, where he would call in the customers by shouting out, "sale day, sale day". 20-30 people would gather on the shop, Alfie and dad would then tray up all the remaining cuts of meat, dress them on the stainless steel trays and knock them out, auction style, for a fiver a tray. This would start people getting in a frenzy, everyone would be calling out for the trays. It was a great way of clearing out the "dlo , or old stock. After this particular knockout finished, June's boyfriend was waiting impatiently by the front doors. It was gone 6pm so we were running behind as it had been a busy day, so the boyfriend beckons June to leave NOW, but Nicky who has started mopping the customer side floor so we can close up, asks the guy to wait outside. He refuses and as nick tries to push him outside, they start to scuffle, the boyfriend grabs nicks work tie and pulling him as nick bundles him out. June is freaking out now, shouting at her guy to stop as both the fellas fall, Nick sticks a couple of punches on June's bloke and then drags him several feet by the scruff of his neck. When he is unceremoniously dumped on his arse in the street, nick closed the concertina doors quickly. The few customers who were still hanging around for a bargain had also quickly moved into Church Street. Within in seconds, June's boyfriend started trying to smash the door windows. As he was being dragged out, he'd got hold of the floor squeegee nick had left propped up on the wall to try and stop being put out. He hit the windows with a massive crash, one went through, the other two were smashed but not fallen out of the window frames. The area seemed to have stopped with all the pandemonium, with people watching from outside the McDonald's restaurant opposite and from the packed bus stops close by. June looked stunned and embarrassed, Alfie approached her telling her to get her coat as he slipped her weeks wages in her hand. The rest of us cleared up the mess, while Nicky and Alfie went to the office at the back of the shop to tell dad what had happened. He had been doing the weekly bookwork, so missed the whole episode. We had to wait around until 8pm before an emergency glazier turned up to board the doors up to make safe and the police came and took statements from the staff. We never saw June again. Me and Ginny meanwhile, had started to get to know each other. Matthews closed its shops on Monday, so we started meeting up on our days off. She was very pretty and had done some modelling for face shots in a couple of magazines as a sixteen year old. We fell in love and dated for just over a year.1982 was another milestone for me, as I passed my driving test at the first time of asking. I used a driving instructor called bob moon who was a strict instructor, but on the back of Alfie and little Dave both passing their tests with him, I didn't hesitate to hire him. 12 lessons and one test in Winchmore Hill later, I was back to the shop and telling everyone of my success. I had recently bought a ford Escort mk1 for £150 from a butcher in the Harlow shop, so I was driving to work the next day. It wouldn't be long before Ron, the newly promoted district manager started sending me to other shops to cover other staff on holiday and others quitting their jobs. In early 1982, the Falklands war had begun, with the United Kingdom protecting its sovereignty against Argentina, who claimed that the islands, which they called "Malvinas, had belonged to them, acquired from the Spanish in the 16th century. Argentina had sent a fleet of vessels along with a landing party of soldiers and shortly after, war between us and the South Americans, began. It was on the two main channels of the time, every day, people were scared for friends and family serving in the armed forces .One of our regular Enfield Town customers told of her worry as her son was serving on HMS Sheffield. We heard the news that it had been struck by an Exocet missile, killing many servicemen, including our customer's son. We all felt a terrible loss for her and the men performing their duty for our country and protecting the lives of the people on the Falkland Islands. It was a strange feeling for me knowing that that lads were fighting for our country in a war, thousands of miles away, while everything seemed normal back in the United Kingdom. Only the news coverage told us otherwise.

CHAPTER 8
On The Road

The chance to work in the Waltham cross branch for a couple of weeks, covering for another butcher who was holiday, was offered to me and as it was only twenty minutes from home, I gladly accepted. Run by Gordon, he was a large ruddy faced gentleman, in his late 50's, he had worked here for over two decades, bringing through Tom Parrish who would become a director of Matthews by the time I joined and jenny, a cashier , who ended up being finance director. Gordon was aided by Peter, another calm, pleasant guy who had been at the Waltham cross as long as his manager. As it was only a couple of miles from home, I would walk or hop on the bus to and from the shop. I loved working there as it was a calm place to learn. The shop wasn't as busy as Enfield, but I had plenty of work to do, with Topbits, ponies, lambs and pigs needing to be cut. These were the days when you could smoke in your workplace and Pete would often be seen rolling up a cigarette and lighting up in between serving and cutting meat. I went back to Enfield after two weeks but it wasn't long before I was away again.

Ron, our district manager, had been instructed to sort out the Archway, North London branch, as sales had dipped and the shop manager was not motivated to do anything about it. Ron called my dad and told him that he wanted me to work with him, boosting the trade if possible to show the manager what could be done with focus and energy. Our first morning didn't get off to the best start, as we travelled towards wood Green, another car pulled out of a side road and t boned us, hitting the driver side , behind Ron and into the rear passenger door and wing. The car spun and we ended 180°, facing where we came from. We were both ok, a little shaken but as soon as details between Ron and the other guy were swapped, we got on our way, the car still able to go. We spent the next two weeks dropping prices and offering promotional products from a bacon and sausage suppliers called Robirch, for virtually cost price. Looking back, it wasn't a surprise we had taken the trade from three thousand pounds per week to six thousand in those two weeks. Unsurprisingly, the trade slipped back to its usual turnover within a month and Johnny the manager was transferred to Crouch End, with Dave who was managing at that branch coming the other way. It was also convenient for the middle management, as they believed that someone was creaming off some meat or money or both as the profit of the shop didn't reflect the prices being charged. I should point out here that branch managers had autonomy when it came to pricing the meat sold in the branch. As long as you turned over a minimum 21 per cent weekly profit, everything was fine. Shop managers were offered two and a half per cent bonus, paid quarterly, on net profit so it was thought to be enough incentive but maybe not enough for some. Dave was reluctant to go as he had been in crouch end for a number of years and built a reputation in the area. He was transferred to Archway where he stayed for the duration of his Matthews career.

CHAPTER 9
Pride Of North London

I was back in Enfield with my usual colleagues and everything with my butchering education was going well. There was always banter within the shop as we were all big football followers with an even split of Arsenal and Tottenham Hotspur fans. I'd loved the Arsenal since I had started following them like my dad. My first encounter with the club was on the television for the 1971 FA cup against Liverpool when Arsenal 2-1 on the day with the winning goal scored by local lad, Charlie George. I later met him in the late seventies, opening a used car dealers showroom in nearby Turnpike Lane, where my dad took me to get his autograph. My grand dad, Arthur, bought my first Arsenal kit with a pair of white football boots like the midfield maestro, Alan Ball. Back in the seventies, football wasn't as readily available as it is today with all the satellite TV sports channels we now have available. We had "match of the day "on Saturday evening but that was too late for me so I would watch "The Big Match" on ITV, on Sunday afternoons and the end of season, FA cup final, which was our only live game. I never went to a live game with dad in the early days, i guess that he wasn't that big a fan as I became and it was me who took him to Highbury for our first match together, watching the then mighty Porto of Portugal, take George graham's team apart, 4-1. It was a shit result but what a great feeling to be standing together at the "Clock End". Back in 1981, Enfield fc had progressed through the preliminary rounds of the FA CUP, getting through to the "proper" 3rd Round where the top division teams are entered into the draw. They had a good team, winning their respective league in recent seasons and at the top end of the league at the time, too. Enfield drew Barnsley fc, a south Yorkshire team managed by the Norman hunter, ex Leeds United and England international legend. The draw was in favour of the non league team, being drawn at Southbury Road, their home ground but the one drawback being the ground couldn't hold much more than one thousand supporters. The club asked the football authority if they could play at either White Hart Lane or Highbury, stadiums of Tottenham and Arsenal respectively as Barnsley Could bring more than double the capacity of Southbury stadium, plus no midweek professional games being played, there could be as many as seven thousand fans wanting to see the game and both clubs could miss out on a big pay day. Myself, Alfie, Nick and young Dave decided that we would go so after finishing work, we jumped on the 29 bus to Wood Green and then walked the rest of the way to white Hart Lane. We could buy tickets at the turnstiles and even though there was a new stand being built with executive boxes, we didn't even think any problems would arise getting in to the ground. Well, we couldn't believe it as we got to end of white Hart Lane and turned right in high street, Tottenham. The footways were packed with fans from Enfield FC, Barnsley, plus Tottenham and Arsenal fans from the local area, to go watch the game. We turned into Paxton Road and queued excitedly to get into the ground. We were struck by the amount of people who had turned out to support Enfield. The public announcer kept telling everyone over the public address system to move forward as more fans wanted to get in to watch the game. Unbelievably, over 30,000 went to watch the game. It was fantastic and though Enfield lost the game that night, they got a rousing cheer and were clapped enthusiastically off the pitch. We left after the game and me and Nick separated from Alfie and Dave and made our way back to our homes. What a night!

CHAPTER 10
Changes

Over the next two years, I built my experience and my confidence, travelling to and working in over a dozen different shops. It was short stints, covering holidays for other staff mainly one week in duration. My first cover as manager came in summer 1983, when I was a confident (read cocky) eighteen year old. Ron the district manager arrived at Enfield and after a few minutes talking to all the staff, disappeared to the office at the back of the shop to see dad. I was called by Ron who then explained I was to cover Rod, the manager at North Wembley, who was about to go on holiday for two weeks and I was to run the shop with the help of the regular shop staff but when I turned up on Tuesday at 6am, that was the last thing on the mind of the assistant manager and the chief cashier who were both in the shop, already working. I took a quick scan of the shop while I got my work coat on and approached the shop window. I asked the assistant manager how the window was laid out and if he would let me know what needed cutting but was met with grunts and muttering under his breath. Anyway it lasted for the rest of the day until everyone realised I was here for the duration and the shop keys were handed over to me reluctantly .The first week we was a couple of hundred quid down but the second week, we took six and a half thousand pounds which was seven hundred up on rod's last week before he went away. I was ecstatic and looking forward to telling my dad how well the shop had done when I got home but he was already asleep as usual in his favourite armchair. He'd been taking this chair for years and it was always the same every Saturday night. He'd have his dinner, a cup of tea and followed up by his silk cut ciggie. And then crash out with his Bobby Charlton comb over hair falling down one side. Me and my brother, mark would see if we could knock it off his head if didn't fall down of its own accord , while he was still asleep It was our only way we could get our own back on the old man for always being a hard bastard to us at work. Every time I went back to Enfield it seemed like a different shop, the "family" was starting to break up and fly the coup. Nicky had gone to the new Safeway superstore that had opened up on Southbury Road, Enfield, close to where he lived, for a bigger pay packet.

Dad had been promoted to assistant district manager. He got a pay rise plus a mark four Ford Cortina as a company car and though he was travelling around quite a bit, I think he enjoyed the prestige of having the new role , along with the new car. Only three years before, he didn't have any money which to this day I don't know what the fuck he was doing with it but anyway, I had saved around £300 in the time I had been working over the previous two years, so after a short discussion, I lent him £120 to buy a 1962 Vauxhall Victor so the family had transport but mainly to get to and from work. He never during his lifetime bought a new car, telling me that he would always prefer a bigger older car rather than its opposite, new small car. With the arrival of the Cortina, he had our current family car, a Triumph 2500 TC, which I thought would be a great car to buy! He said I would have to pay him £300, so as I didn't have all the money and I wanted the car, I got a loan from the provident. The Triumph was a lovely car but wasn't a smart move for my finances as it drunk petrol, with me spending £50 per week, which was two thirds of my weekly salary which was £75 after tax but it was a great car for my young ego. Little Dave, now was getting his chance at management and like me was in and out of Enfield branch, managing other shops while the regular management were on vacation. At 21, he got his first permanent shop manager role in Kilburn, North West London. It was a new unit, trading as Eat-E-Nuf, a market style trading shop, with a pile it high, sell it cheap ethos. It fitted well into the area which was a predominantly Irish and Caribbean community, with big families, low income, competing with Corrigan's, an established Irish butcher. My brother, mark, would also start his full time career at Kilburn.

CHAPTER 11
Young Turks

Kilburn was to become a big part of my life for many reasons, leaving an indelible mark until this day, as I write this book. And for my brother mark too. Mark who is two years my junior, had learned the basics of butchery at Enfield Town while I was starting to work at other shops. He left school early in his last year there as he was a problem to the teaching staff, and as he had a job, it was agreed that he didn't need to stay the last few months as he wouldn't be completing all his exams. He had to tread the same path as me, being the yob, taking the shit treatment but luckily, working for an easy going manager in Alfie, and a supportive colleague in Dave. They bonded over the months and when Kilburn Eat E Nuf opened and bombed, business wise, young Dave was given his shot. Mark and Dave worked hard and had support through three other full time staff plus a sixteen year old Saturday girl, Debbie, who was later to become my girlfriend then wife for Thirteen years.

The district manager for Eat E Nuf was a guy called Johnny who was helping Dave build up the trade in Kilburn, working in the shop a couple of times per week. In hindsight, Johnny wasn't the sharpest tool in the shed and when he was teaching my 16 year old brother that meat could be cut on a bandsaw with no hand guard much quicker, there would be trouble ahead. Sure enough, I got a call one afternoon while working in Archway shop that my brother had an accident. He'd been cutting frozen lamb loins, his hand had slipped and due to no hand guard available, his hand was pulled into the blade and it ripped his little finger off. He was taken by ambulance to St Mary's hospital in Paddington. His finger couldn't be saved and he was out of work for 3 months. It took five years of fighting the insurance company to get him compensation and it went to getting an offer on the day of the hearing, on the steps of the court. I went back to Enfield to support Alfie, who was now the shop manager plus we had a whole new team of staff to bed in. Our middle chain of management changed too. Tom, the area manager had retired and was replaced by Brian, who was an experienced Matthews man who would also give me plenty of opportunities to work at other shops and allow me to develop my knowledge. Meanwhile, I was getting to know the staff in Enfield especially Lesley, a young woman from Harlow, who was in a relationship with the Waltham Abbey shop manager while working there but had a bust up with him and got a transfer to Enfield. Our new recruits included Karen who had come from the same council estate where I grew up. She was a couple of years younger than me but I had seen her playing with the other kids on the streets running through the development. The other new member was Kevin who we nicknamed "Magnus", after the television boffin, Magnus Pike. Kevin would wave his arms about vigorously whenever he was talking, like the television celebrity, so he got the new moniker. We all bonded very quickly and supported Alfie, who was a natural manager of people. It was during this time that I had moved out of my home and rented a flat above a barber shop in Enfield Highway, just a mile or so from where I had previously lived, so I was familiar with the area. I shared the two bedroom home with a guy who I had known for a couple of years, who I had met through my network of friends.

During another managerial stint at Archway, I was faced with a major dilemma. This was a shop where it was considered unsafe to take the daily takings to the bank, so the cash and cheques were collected by a company called Silver Shield. The takings were put in a leather wallet and a plastic seal placed with a numerical code, fitted in the slot provided on the top of the opening so it could easily be seen if it had been tampered with. The security guard turned up at the usual time one afternoon, he collecting the takings along with the tally of the total amount inside the wallet, while returning another one with the previous chitty, stamped as acknowledgement of receiving the last banking. When I opened the wallet to get the receipt out, my jaw dropped when I saw what turned out to be two thousand, three hundred pounds, still inside the wallet with a stamped slip for the banking. Somebody had

Fucked up big time and my mind was torn. Do I keep the money and say nothing or inform senior management? I phoned my dad for advice on what I should do. He immediately told me to ring head office, which I did, who then informed the company chief cashier. I was instructed to put the money filled wallet in the fridge and lock it as we had no safe in the shop, where it would be collected from the following morning. I received a thank you but no reward for my honesty. Nothing was ever mentioned again. I wonder what happened to that money?

Chapter 12
Camden Town

I went back to Camden Town after Richard the manager was sacked and was replaced by Brian. I ended up working there for the whole summer of 1984. It was a great experience, seeing the different people pulled to this area, with its rich fashion and music culture.

The shop was bang opposite Camden market, where the drifting aroma of weed could be smelt through the day. It was a quiet shop trade -wise, taking around £4,000 per week but it was never dull. We had the TVAM studios just down the road, so we were regularly visited by Rustie Lee, the breakfast show chef, who would buy her cuts of meat from us, to cook on her section of the show. Rustie was famous for her loud laugh as well as her cooking, it was so infectious whenever she was in the shop, we would all be laughing with her. We would be visited by the television celebrities and pop stars of the day, who would have been recording in the Hawley road studios and then some would drop in and buy meat from us. I recollect asking jenny, the beautiful vocalist from the Belle stars (eighties' pop band), out for a date but she politely declined. A short walk away from the shop was Arlington House, made famous in the song" One Better Day" by the pop group, Madness. This place was a hostel for the homeless in the area, attracting many interesting characters, mainly losing the battle against alcohol and drugs. One particular person from Arlington was Mary, who would walk around Camden high street with the aid of a Zimmer frame and a bottle of spirit tucked away in her pocket. She was well known in the area and amongst her peers and shopkeepers. One particular Day, we noticed her approaching the entrance to the shop so Brian signalled to me to duck below the counter and watch as Mary entered slowly on her walking frame. She looked around what appeared to be an empty shop and then without any delay, put the frame aside and we watched gobsmacked as she walked unaided and with no apparent problem towards our display cabinet, opening one of many carrier bags stuffed in her cardigan pocket and started filling it with our meat! Brian jumped up, shouting at Mary, "what the fuck are you doing?". I almost pissed myself laughing as she dropped the bag, told Brian to "fuck off" and scrambled out of the shop, dragging the frame behind her. One evening, me and Brian had finished the day, pulled down the shutter, locked up and walked over to Barclays Bank to put the days takings placed in a large leather purse style moneybag, into the night safe, situated in the wall of the building and used when the bank was closed. As we walked back towards the shop and where our cars were parked, we spotted a drunk woman leaning against our shop shutter. We approached the doorway to see what she was doing and asked her the same. She was so fucking drunk that she couldn't talk, only slur as we watched as a puddle of piss appear at her feet as she urinated in her polyester trousers, the piss patch in her crutch area, a tell- tale sign!

Camden has always been a centre for musical creativity, with many famous bands of the time playing at the "ELECTRIC BALLROOM" which was situated across the road from our shop, amongst them were The Smiths, who

I discovered while still being a big fan of all things electronic, bands like Depeche Mode, New Order, Human league and Kraftwerk. There was followers of all different types of music that were drawn to this area ,with the varied music venues on offer in the area such as Camden Palace and Dublin Castle, to name just two. It made for a colourful and vibrant place and where I would spend my weekends with friends, drinking and smoking weed.

A couple of other Matthews shops where I had brief stints was Acton and Borehamwood. Old oak common lane in Acton was just off the main arterial road A40, so it was never going to be busy , it was another of the units taken over by Matthews from the Williams bros chain and was managed by Bert. I only worked there for a week for holiday cover but it was the quirky drinks cabinet, Bert had in the shop. Now, it's not advisable to drink while using sharp knives but he obviously liked a drink as I stumbled over his hidden stash, one afternoon. There was a chest freezer in the back of the shop that had milk crates stacked on top of it and being an inquisitive type, I removed the crates and opened the lid to find several bottles of gin and tonic and one single glass. I was taken aback by my find but on the Saturday on my final day, everything became clear. As the day came to an end, Burt opened up his drinks cabinet, pour himself a G & T, relieved he'd got through another week.

Meanwhile at Borehamwood, Stan the Matthews shop manager had his own secret stash but it wasn't in a decommissioned chest freezer. I went to the storeroom to get a ball of string to tie up a few roles of topside and silverside beef and came across his library of pornographic magazines, there were hundreds! I didn't say anything to Stan when I walked out of the storeroom but I was amazed at the volume of different publications he had obviously collected over the years. I guess his wife wasn't happy having them at home so he decided to store them at work. I was going to different branches every other week it seemed during 1984. A two week stint at Greenford started rather frosty when Stevie Edwards who was an experienced butcher from Barnet, was sent by the area manager to support me as staff was thin on the ground, with three staff absent, leaving two elderly members to run the branch. On the first morning, I arrived at 6am, meeting Reg who was the assistant manager. He'd worked at Greenford for several years and worked as a butcher for five decades. A lovely fella he wasn't taken with Steve when he bowled in a little while after me. He was a short guy who was a huge fan of bodybuilding, modelling himself on Mike Mentzer, an American Mr Olympia, at his peak in the 1970's. He had a large thick moustache that Stevie had imitated and though only five and a half foot tall, he was huge sideways, with an impressive muscular build. But he was fucking annoying, being an obsessed Stevie Wonder fan , believing he could sing like the Motown legend , he would stop anyone near him and sing at them, even if you didn't want to hear it.

The three of us got to work on the display which took a couple of hours to complete. With the show ready for customers and passing trade to purchase our lovely cuts of meat, we opened the door, waiting to do business. Sheila, the cashier arrived, who was introduced by Reg, made her way to the back of the shop. She screamed loudly running out of the ladies toilet. Steve turned to me and grinned; "I've left my calling card in her toilet, I've done a big shit and left it in the pan" Thankfully, he was moved to another shop within two days.

CHAPTER 13
Opportunities

March 1985, I done my first week over in South Oxhey, Watford, working with Dave and his team who had been working together for a few years, so everything ran smoothly. They sold a lot of offal, which if you don't know, are the internal organs, liver, kidneys and heart. These are very cheap to buy and Dave had tapped into the massive dog ownership that was especially prevalent at this time in the Mid Eighties. It was driven by the unemployed incumbents of South Oxhey, who were breeding dogs as a form of income, mainly Bull terriers and Rottweiler's as they fetched big money. I was told by Brian and Ron, my line managers, that Dave was moving to Devon and that this was my opportunity to run my own shop. They told me that I would work with Dave, learning as much as I could in the shortest amount of time as he'd been waiting to hear about his new home in Newton Abbot and finally got it at short notice. The plan was a bit half arsed but I got in, done my week watching and listening and then on Saturday afternoon, Dave handed me the shop keys. St. Andrews Square, South Oxhey, is a large residential development, resided by mainly working class people. The shop was positioned half way down one side of the shopping area, which looked jaded and was in need of a refurbishment. The shop had received a makeover in the previous 12 months, in the red and blue wall panels that were the choice of colour scheme to complement the company fascia. It was taking around £6000 per week and was highly profitable. It was staffed by mick, Darren, Graham, Mandy, Cathy plus myself now. Mick was in his 40's and hoped he was taking over the shop. He'd been relief manager for a few years, mainly covering the smaller William bros shops, that was part of Borthwick group's retail division. I never spoke to him about the position of Oxhey manager and his desire to be manager because I didn't have the knowledge or the social skills at nineteen, just aware of myself and my needs. I fitted in quickly, taking everything I had learned to that point in my career and got about running the shop. Graham and Darren were a similar age to me, Mandy was 17, while Mick and Cathy were both in their mid-forties, so a division between us occurred and i soon realised that mick was pissed off about me being manager. He was still doing his relief work, working in Oldfield circus every Monday unlike the Matthews shops which closed on that day, mick picking up a regular extra boost to his weekly salary. Our Wealdstone branch became manager-less soon after, mick applied for the role and soon got his wish to be a manager in his own right. Cathy became less hostile towards me and we had a happy camp. My personal life was changing too, as I had started seeing Mandy, having sex with her after we had finished work on a regular basis as we had fancied each other as soon as we clapped eyes. This had happened within a few weeks of us starting to work together but it was a problem as I had struck up a relationship with Debbie, the cashier from Kilburn, so decided to cool it with Mandy. I took Debbie for a couple of dates and we got on really well. We'd arranged for me to make my first visit to her family home, where I would meet her mum and dad. I'd bought us a bottle of wine that I gave her on a previous date to take home and we would have a drink when I arrived. I finished work on the Saturday afternoon, bought a bunch of flowers and set of down the M1 motorway towards Willesden. It was the weekend of the band aid concerts in nearby Wembley and Philadelphia in the United States, and the weather was glorious. The sun was shining and I was excited to see deb again after finishing work for the day. I approached her house and rung the bell, and was greeted by Deb. I looked inside the long hallway and a telephone stand fixed on the wall had something sitting on it that was familiar to me. As I crossed the threshold I looked closely and realised it was the bottle of wine I had bought and given to Deb on our previous date. It was fucking empty! I looked to left into the doorway of the living room and slumped in the armchair, was deb's dad, pissed has he had necked the whole bottle of drink. I was furious but as she took me to the kitchen to meet her mum, I was told he had a drink problem. The alcohol "problem" was to be a spectre in our relationship for the next twelve years.

CHAPTER 14
Shit Hits The Fan

I'd settled in at South Oxhey and the summer went well, business wise. We were making a profit and I was earning small amounts of commission, paid quarterly. I was back at mum and dads home after my flat sharer bailed out and moved in to his boyfriends place and left me with the £50 per week, rent. I couldn't afford it, even on my £110 weekly wage. I approached dad and asked if I could move back in to the family home in Waltham Gardens. *"You will have to ask your mum"* was the stock answer I always got from him whenever it was something he didn't want to deal with. *"It's okay with me"* he said with a rye smile. Me and Debbie had become a full blown relationship and we started seeing each other regularly. She had quit her Job in Kilburn and got an office role in a builder's merchants, close to her home. She would work Monday to Friday and every other Saturday, I would nip out of the shop and drive to her home, pick her up and bring her back to the shop. We were so horny for each other, I would pull in to a sheltered parking area and we would have sex then get back to work.

The rest of 1985 went well, I even traded in my old Volvo 144 for a Rover sd1 3.5 V8 saloon car. It was way too big a car for me but I always wanted a V8 and even though it was several years old, it looked and ran well. I took a two week vacation in April 1986, travelling to the south coast with Debbie for a few days in Boscombe and then the rest of the break was spent between Willesden and Enfield. Ron, the district manager was running the shop while I was away and when I went back to work on Tuesday, he was there to meet me. *"We went for the trade but lost some profit"*, Ron said. *"I've bumped the stock up but if you put your prices up this week, you will cover some of the losses"*, he went on. It turned out by going for the trade he'd dropped 15% gross profit, turning in 10% instead. He'd fucked up and I had to carry the can. The shit got even worse when the new area manager turned up at the shop on Wednesday afternoon. He had been dropped into our area for a direct swap for Brian, the previous area manager. It seemed like I've been fitted up when he asked Graham and Darren to do a stock check, closing the shop an hour early. When the manager got the figures and they were about a £700 disparity from the weekend figures Ron had posted ten days previously, I tried to remain calm outside but I was freaking out inside my head. The rest of the staff was sent home and I stood alone with Bill, the area manager. He asked for the shop keys and told me to go home and stay there until I would receive a letter from head office. I had two weeks off and broke out in a rash which apparently was brought on by stress during by my enforced *"holiday"*, well that's what the doctor said! The letter I was waiting for turned up after a few days and I was asked to go to head office in Smithfield and meet the human resources manager, Roger. I jumped on the bus for my day of execution as I suspected that I would be losing my role as manager best case or sacked. During the time I was off, Ron didn't call to apologise or help. I guess he was keeping his head down.

I got off the bus close to Smithfield market and walked towards my destiny, up at St. John's Lane. I entered through the main door and approached the reception. *"I'm here to see Mister Parsons, I have an appointment"*. The receptionist was pleasant and pointed towards his door. When I knocked and entered his office, Roger greeted me with a warm welcome, asking me to sit opposite him at his desk. Roger spoke with an educated accent as he read a brief synopsis of what had happened, a report compiled by the area manager and asked me for my thoughts. I'd decided beforehand that I was going to fall on my own sword and offer to stand down from management. *Fuck that shit I thought* I guessed I would be sacked so if I resigned from my position as manager I might save my job at Matthews and get a butchery role somewhere on our district, closer to home.

CHAPTER 15
Happy Hammersmith

I had indeed surprised the HR manager, as he seemed lost for words because I took the wrap for the loss of profit and dodgy figures and not dropped Ron in the crap. He told me to go to Eat e Nuf in North End Road, Fulham, report to Tony who was the area manager's younger brother. Was I surprised when I saw him the following week. He was about five and a half foot in height, with bright bleach blonde hair, tattoos covered his hands and neck. He turned out to be a decent fella, working hard to integrate me with the other staff in the shop. A week went by and I was told to go to Matthews in king Street, Hammersmith. The manager was Steve, a tall, thin guy who had worked at the biggest Matthews shop in size and trade in Surrey Street, Croydon. It was turning over more than two million pounds per year which was a fantastic amount for the time. Hammersmith was the complete opposite of Fulham, which was small and scruffy. This shop was relatively new, open for just a short time, furthermore, it was massive! The floor on the customer's side at the front was bigger than the whole work area of our Fulham branch. The main window display was about ten feet long and swept into the shop, with a twenty foot serve over counter, fitted with external refrigeration which keeps the inside of a shop cooler as there is no build- up of heat from the motors and finished with the latest Italian styled curved glass. On the Opposite side to the counters stood one large open multi deck display unit that covered the whole of the other main wall. On the last wall that created the customer shopping area was a beautiful delicatessen counter, which had its own red and white striped Dutch canopy, emblazoned with DELICATESSEN. For me, this was the pinnacle in shop selling areas, free standing baskets, full of dried goods, waiting to be picked up as an extra sale by the customers in the store. Behind the counters was even more space than I'd seen in any of the shops I had worked in over the previous five years. To the right were two large walk in chillers and one freezer, integrated with slick sliding doors which were covered in a protective red metal coating, matching the exterior refrigerator walls. To the left as walked towards the rear of the shop was fully tiled in dark blue, punctuated by mirrored stainless steel sheets where the prep areas were for cutting the sides of beef, lamb and pork carcase. At the end of the row of the three 4 'x 2 ' cutting blocks , there was a two foot gap and there stood this beautiful purpose built modular table with a state of the art label printer manufactured by Bizerba, a German company which is one of the finest quality producers out there. I'd never used one, I'd never seen one, as I always had to hand write labels for packs of meat, that had started to take off in butchers shops. Next was an industrial band saw that was so big it had safety rails fitted around it. Steve had his own office opposite the band saw and the large staffroom even had separate toilet cubicles with 3 separate units for both sexes. Shit, this place was awesome! Hammersmith was staffed by Steve the manager and 10 staff, aged between seventeen and twenty five and it buzzed with youthful fun. On my first day of work, I reported to Steve who told me to break down a couple of beef forequarters, to steakout for the window trays. He was a dour person who I would find out was bored with his role at the shop, looking for a busier role after being the assistant manager at Surrey Street in Croydon. Being at the king Street shop was great and the week flew by owing to the fact that I was cutting plenty of carcase meat along with Darren and Marvin, who had recently transferred from Clapham Junction branch. The following Tuesday, I was back with Billy and his team at eat e nuf in North end road. There was a new butcher who had started while I was in Hammersmith and he turned up with a small two knife holster fixed to a belt around his waist which was the funniest thing to me at the time. It seemed weird to be carrying a ten inch polyurethane block strapped to your leg and waist! We all got to work on the display, me and the new man, Kevin, cutting the meat for the tray display that goes in the window. I always liked cutting the beef and lamb trays as there were more cuts and a higher degree of difficulty in displaying the steaks to make them look nice to my eye and hopefully, the customers. So between me doing the beef and lamb, Kevin was cutting the whole chicken up for breast and legs. He then had to bust up a pig. You get the belly, loin chops, spare rib or sometimes called shoulder chops, tenderloin and rump. There are plenty of great cuts from the pig. The display took two hours to complete between me, Tony and Kevin, with the shop opening for customers at 8.30am. We cracked on, getting meat prepped for the day and the following couple. Everything was going well and I tried to break the ice with Kevin who had been working quietly during the morning. We chatted when I asked about where he worked previously and he told me Dewhurst in Fulham but had left because he had fallen out with the shop manager. We worked until lunchtime and Kevin asked Tony if he could pop out to get a bite to eat. He slipped out in his white work coat and we never saw him again that day. In fact, we didn't see him again until some two weeks later, when he walked in unannounced but I will save that for later in a following chapter! The following week, I was working back in Hammersmith again, this time I was working with Richard, who had recently been made district manager in West London and was also my old District Manager, Ron's brother. Richard was running the king Street shop while Steve was taking his annual holiday. Matthews had been having a recruitment drive at the time because as proved by my toing and froing, staff levels were down.

CHAPTER 16
Decisions Too Be Made

While I had been working in Fulham, the king Street shop had taken a couple of new butchers, both of them leaving their posts at Dewhurst. John was an amiable chap of Irish descent from white city and Gary, a heavy set guy who came from Fulham. Richard was doing his best to boost sales, getting us to cut lots of meat and sell it cheap, as was the trading style of Matthews. He was an ebullient guy and sometimes he let excitement get the better of him! He would shout loudly, double entendres, or role play two characters, himself and normally a female customer, talking in a middle class, high pitched accent. Or he would just loudly say "I'm as happy as a dog with two dicks". If it was quiet, in the shop and street he would say "Are they all cardboard cut outs or just tumbleweed blowing in the wind!"

Gary meanwhile, was turning out to be a stand-off guy, not talking to the rest of the staff. He looked so bloody miserable, like he didn't want to be there. Richard wasn't having him not being part of the team and decided to play a prank. While Gary was sitting in a toilet cubicle having a shit , Richard called me and John to follow him while he carried a foam filled fire extinguisher to the toilets, kicked the door open and covered Gary in foam while the poor sod was sitting on the bog! Gary rose calmly, covered in foam, pulled his trousers up, pushed pass us and walked into the changing area of the staff room. He hung up his white coat, put on his overcoat and walked out of the shop not uttering a word. How Richard didn't get beaten up or worse for this prank, I'll never know. Everyone went back to doing their work, not quite sure what to say. The rest of the week passed without any more drama apart from me slicing the top of my thumb open which required stitching, when I was speeding through five forequarters of beef, waiting to be boned out.

I was back to Fulham again the following week and everything was cool and calm. Another couple of weeks passed, I was cutting a few lambs in preparation for Friday and Saturday, when who should walk in but Kevin and Gary! They stunk of beer, looked drunk and probably were stoned too. All the staff stood still Looking at them, then Kevin without warning, pulled out a butchers steak knife from inside his coat and shouted at me. Oi, you, come outside, I want to fucking have it out with you! I didn't know what I'd bloody done but I kept calm and said " I'm busy at the moment, come back later!" He replied he'd be back when the shop was closed and both guys walked off. I didn't hang around as you might expect I turned to Tony and said I wasn't waiting around to get stabbed up and got the fuck out of there as quickly as I could. To this day, I don't recollect saying anything out of order but I soon found out that these two fellas had alcoholism and possibly mental health issues too.

I travelled back to Hammersmith, telling Richard, who was still running the shop during Steve's vacation, that those two piss heads had pulled a knife on me. I found a clean white coat and got on with some cutting.

The weekend came round and Saturday was as busy as usual, particularly around lunchtime, when out of the blue, Kevin and Gary walked in the shop, pissed up and mouthing off obscenities and pointing towards Richard. They both approached the counter, pushing customers out of the way who were being served or waiting for their purchases to be handed over, launched the liquid from the beer cans they were both holding in the direction of everyone working in the vicinity of Richard. Everyone ducked out of the way apart from Richard because he was about twenty stone, who couldn't move quick enough and got covered in what turned out to be piss.

Meanwhile, despite all the drama going on at work, Debbie and myself had by now moved into our second year of a growing relationship. Even though I was still nineteen and she had only just turned eighteen years old, we talked about getting a home together. The need for getting a place together was intensified when Deb had told me she was pregnant. Oh fuck we didn't plan that! We were irrational in not using contraception as we were indoctrinated by our catholic upbringing and took too many risks having unprotected sex. Deb's mum and dad wouldn't let us live together unless we got married but we wasn't thinking of tying the knot so we took the decision that she would have to have an abortion. I made discreet inquiries and found Marie Stopes pregnancy clinics. We talked it over, made appointments and went over to Buckhurst Hill where the operation took place. We never told anyone and neither brought it up between us.

CHAPTER 17
Coming To Power

The next couple of months were calm, I'd been transferred to King Street permanently, Steve was back managing and apart from a couple of departures and new staff being integrated, the shop ran like clockwork. Rumours started circulating that J H Dewhurst were about to acquire the whole of Matthews but I was arrogant and egotistical not to believe what was being said as I thought that Matthews was too good to be run by a "shit company like them!". However, it came to pass during 1986 that Dewhurst did take over the company and there was major upheaval as the Matthews shops had to change to the new administration. Middle chain management were made redundant as the Matthews shops became integrated into the new structure, but as it turned out, was good fortune for me. Steve, the Hammersmith shop manager was promoted within weeks of meeting our new district and area managers. Peter, our new district manager, a Dewhurst man, came and chatted to me, asking if I would be interested in taking over king Street after management training at the Waterloo training centre. Of course I was, so a week later, off I went. Upon returning to King Street, I talked to Steve and we discussed the situation of our changing roles, both of us looking forward to the new challenges ahead. Within a few weeks, Steve was gone, in his new role as assistant district manager. I never spoke to or saw him again. Meanwhile, Peter smith the new DM, was in place with me at king Street. We got on immediately and working with him was really enjoyable. He was very calm and got his message across about how he expected me to run the shop. I took the manager role in early 1987, which was a massive year in my personal and working life. I stayed at king Street for another four months, until I got an offer to work with an old work colleague and early life mentor, Ron Jarvis, who had left Matthews and started his own butchers in a residential area of Luton. He had moved to Milton Keynes which had been designated as an area for massive development with lots of new homes for first time buyers. I explained to Debbie that Ron had offered me a job and that we should look at Milton Keynes for a place to buy because it would be much cheaper to get a step on the housing ladder than it would be in London; Ron had been banging on about how great this area was going to be. He had a young family and they had recently moved from Stevenage to improve their surroundings. We decided to drive the fifty miles up the M1 motorway. I took off one Sunday morning with Debbie as we had discussed earlier in the week that it would be great idea to look around the area where Ron lived, viewing a selection of homes that might be a place to start living together. We set off from Willesden on the one hour trip towards junction fourteen of the M1 motorway, navigating the road grid system of Milton Keynes, getting lost as every bloody road looked the same until we came the town that gave us the best British sports car, the Aston Martin, as I'd found myself in Tickford street in Newport Pagnell which was a bonus for a car nut like me. I drove away from the old town, speeding down the single carriageway when we approached signs advertising new starter homes in the North East of the city called Willen Park so I took a sharp exit right, turning into a building site. Avoiding some dodgy iron work on the unfinished access road in our old Ford Capri, we followed the for sale signs in to Bells Meadow. Turning into the small cul de sac, I pointed the steering wheel into the right bend of the road where our future home stood, sitting in the corner, timber trim adorned its façade, small front garden, full of flowering shrubs. We felt full of excitement while walking around the outside of the property, looking through the glazed kitchen door at the rear .There was a small fitted kitchen with tiled splash back and brown linoleum flooring to match the magnolia walls. The rear garden was massive despite looking like a triangular piece of cheese due to being on a corner plot. I was a shit gardener because I was fucking lazy when it came to all things horticultural unlike my dad who had tried his hand at being a landscape gardener in the seventies and later constantly worked in the family garden in Waltham gardens, on his weekends off. We both liked the house so went to the sales office and made enquiries. Leaving our contact details, we left to find Ron's home. This place was a far cry from the flat I had broken into a lived in for a while, above a Matthews shop in Saint Albans Road, Watford a year or so before. I had worked in the shop for a couple of days in the winter of 1984, discovered that there was an empty property above, so decided to investigate. Within days, I forced entry into the vacant flat, bringing with me all my possessions that amounted to a folding bed and my portable electronic keyboard, (still had dreams of being in a band),a sack full of clothes plus a new lock for the front door. I couldn't afford curtains or more likely had no idea to put them up, so covered the two ground floor windows with black dustbin liners so no-one could see in. This was how I lived for a couple of months until I returned one evening from work to find the doors and windows boarded up with a note from the Hertfordshire constabulary to pick up my belongings from Watford police station. I was questioned by a police officer how I had got in to the maisonette, duly warned and got off with a caution and informing Matthews head office of my misdemeanour. I did get a written warning from the bosses but nothing else was said.

CHAPTER 18
Luton And Beyond

So I get an offer to work with my old Matthews boss, Ron. He's opening his own shop after initially being demoted to shop manager in Stevenage close to where he lived with his wife and young son after the restructuring of Matthews in the aftermath of the Dewhurst buy out from Borthwick's. He had been told he had no future with our new employees, so after a couple of months of looking at various locations, he found an empty butcher shop in Marsh Farm , a working class housing estate in a suburb of Luton. The majority of people in Marsh Farm relied on the two main sources of income if you lived there. Vauxhall Motors, which was situated near Luton Airport, or the benefits office.

He contacted me by phone at first and offered a job in his aggressive, fist pumping style. Initially, I was hesitant because I had a great shop in Hammersmith and I was very happy. "Come and work for me, don't be a cunt and let me down, unless you can't handle the work that is." Ron sensed my lack of desire to change a good thing, however I was torn as the change in job could mean I could buy my own house and at some point, live with Debbie. He knew full well that I was a grafter and he needed to get staff he could trust but still wanted to try and wind me up. "Stay a Dewhurst wanker" he said, trying to provoke me. I agreed to meet him at his home in Milton Keynes and talk further about his offer. I was excited for the opportunity to work with him as I believed it would improve my skills and experience, learning as much as possible from Ron. A short time after the first visit to Milton Keynes, I drove to Ron's house again, we spoke with excitement about us working together again and the informal meeting ended with me being offered another fifty pound per week more than my salary with Matthew's and me accepting the opportunity for a new challenge. I went back to work the following Tuesday, handing in my notice to quit. My career at Matthews had lasted eight years, from April, nineteen seventy nine until May, nineteen eighty seven and had worked in over twenty different shops in London and Hertfordshire. I worked with many wonderful people who taught me a skill for life, something I could always return to if I ever I left the trade to pursue another career.

Debbie and I went back to see the house builders in Milton Keynes and put down the deposit of ninety nine pounds sterling to hold that little two bed home and then almost forgetting that we had to instruct a solicitor to purchase it until two weeks later when I got a call from the sales guys at Willen Park, asking who would we be using to sort out the conveyancing. This happened because both our own parent's had lived in council houses so we never got the advice that would of helped us in the situation we were in. We applied with the Abbey National for the mortgage and after a couple of interviews with the mortgage specialist we received the good news that we could borrow one hundred per cent of the cost of buying the house which was thirty nine thousand, nine hundred and ninety five pounds. After several weeks, I received the keys and moved in alone during August nineteen eighty seven. I slept on the new sofa that was so big, one of the corner units had to go in the cupboard under the stairs because it didn't fit in the living room. It looked great in the bloody warehouse showroom. Shit, I really made some fucking stupid decisions, I was so naïve! I started working with Ron and Phil, who was another ex-employee of Matthews, previously working in Bletchley. Fat Phil as he was known, was your stereotypical butcher. Large and loud with short ginger hair, the fella was a grafter and a damn good butcher to boot. Ron decided to open with a bang by going full blaze on the amount of meat he ordered. We were to open on a Wednesday, that being a market day with loads of stalls surrounding the shopping area beneath the block of flats, which was a large area and People flocked from all over this part of Luton to grab a bargain. We cut ten forequarters and five topbits of beef, once they were cut, were meticulously trimmed and hung in the fridge with steaks, ribs and rolls hooked on to the fridge walls in such a way that anyone would think we had OCD, meats from the right side of the cow on one wall, the left side on another wall. The pigs and lambs were broken down and placed on their own walls, legs, shoulders and loins all hanging in the same direction, we could of sold the meat from the cold room, the display was so good. So we could stock the display cabinets quickly with the boneless meats for steaks and dicing, we had stainless steel trays on rolling trollies, layering all the small pieces and trimmed offcuts in them, which made things easier and a time saver as this was a long shop. Posters were placed on the front shutter, announcing our imminent opening, we were buzzing with excitement on the opening day. Ron picked me and Phil up who also lived in Milton Keynes, at five am and we headed off southbound towards Marsh Farm. We put on a fantastic show, there was meat everywhere. With opening time approaching, there was banging on the front shutter and we could hear people calling out to be let in. As we raised the shutter, it was incredible to be met by a throng of people, approaching sixty in number, all wanting to come into R J Jarvis Quality Meats. Needless to say, we had incredibly busy day, taking more money in that day than the previous butcher had in one week of trading. The shop proved to be a roaring success in those first few months and we were exhausted at the end of every day, working flat out for eleven hours with just a coffee and a quick fag break in between busy spells, not stopping to eat. No wonder we all lost weight!

In November nineteen eighty seven and after two and a half years of dating, Debbie and I got married. We begged, stole and borrowed what we could to have our big day, along with two thousand pounds that we managed to save. Debbie borrowed her older sister, Jackie's wedding dress, me buying an off the peg suit from Alfred Dunn's. A family friend had an old Bentley limousine that he kindly drove Debbie to church in. We got married in Mary Magdalene in Willesden, North West London on a grey Saturday morning. The church was full, with family members from both sides, apart from my brother who decided to disappear in the week leading up to the wedding, when he was supposed to be my best man. One of my two closest friends, Danny, stood in at the last moment. I would be eternally grateful to the man. Debbie's older sibling Jackie and deb's twin sister Kay along with my sister Sam were the bridesmaids. The service seemed to go on forever and I was relieved when it was over, looking forward to moving on to the fun part. The Piss-up. We held the reception above a pub in Wembley, the manager of the pub decorating the rooms we used in bunting and congratulation posters for free as he knew a load of Irishmen would be coming to drink his pub dry. Our two mums with the help of other family members knocked up the tonne of egg mayonnaise and tin salmon and cucumber sandwiches for the hundred or so congregation, including the young priest who married us. This was the first chance to see my Nan, Elsie, since the funeral of my Granddad Jim, who had passed away in July of that year. It was a fantastic day, lasting for several hours, most of us steaming drunk. There wasn't enough money left to go on honeymoon, so we went back to Melda and Paddy's house for our first night as Mister and Misses Bye. We stayed in West London the following day and the drink flowed all day in the local working man's club, where the family congregated once again to toast this young couple. Now Debbie would be allowed to move in our house in Bells Meadow with me and we couldn't be happier.

Chapter 19
The Harder I Try

November is normally a shit month for trade in the meat game because everyone is pulling in their belts, saving hard earned money for loved ones presents at Christmas time , However we wasn't standing about scratching our arses. Business was brisk due to us being ultra-competitive in our prices and the three of being focussed all the time. It was tiring physically and mentally, no time to switch off, the people in Marsh Farm were ready for a fast ready money trading business like ours, top quality meat along with family friendly prices, the queues for our products were relentless.

December trade built to a crescendo, we worked every day in the last couple of weeks leading up to Christmas Eve. The side of my right hand was sore and swollen red from all the hundreds of topsides and silverside beef rolls that had to be hand tied. And then there was the bloody turkeys! Ron didn't buy any eviscerated birds, only guts in, known in the trade as New York Dressed. They look fantastic when there is big display of creamy white Yetruks, white feathered and the fattier, tastier bronze and black Kelly birds that originally came from Ireland, hanging on the rails around a shop however the smaller hen birds are a sod to clean. Making a small incision around the arse, you have to cut deep enough into the fat to get your fingers in but making sure the hole that is being created to get a hand in the cavity is not too big that the turkey cannot be stuffed. A hand is pushed inside right up into the ribcage, pulling all the innards out, hopefully intact, without splitting the spleen, which can stain the meat green if it torn. Don't split the skin. Christmas Eve was manic, trade was fantastic and after finishing a sixteen hour day, Ron gave us a small cash bonus and a big bag of scoff including a turkey for the Christmas day. We got five days off which we would need to recover after the intensity of working ninety hours in the last week at the shop.

I drove down to Willesden with Deb, on Christmas Eve night, both of us looking forward to spending time with her family, eating lots and getting pissed. We divided the next few days between Belton Road , the Working-Mans club in the High Road and Waltham Gardens with my Mum, Dad, Mark and Sam.

After the Christmas break, I returned to work fully refreshed and ready for what nineteen eighty eight would bring me and Deb plus the hard work in the shop as we pushed to get the sales up and Ron pushed me and Phil to the limit, buying more and more meat from our main meat supplier, Snelsons, a meat wholesaler from Leicester. Ron had managed to get four weeks credit from Snellys' as we'd called them, allowing him to use the money that had been accumulated through the shop sales to purchase other suppliers products where there was no credit account, thus getting a degree of trust by paying cash and then asking for a payment holiday. This would usually amount to between two and four weeks, depending on the size of the company, financially. This was my first lesson in OPM, otherwise known as other people's money. With the money leveraged, Ron started investing in the shop, first buying chest freezers and then updating the rear of the shop with latest hygienic wall cladding and refrigeration. It all looked good, the shop immaculately clean and modern. With the investment along with all our combined drive and determination, the shop turnover grew rapidly, with a One Hundred Per Cent in revenue within the first twelve months. I was disappointed not to get an increase in my salary after the first year, especially as there was a massive increase in trade and Ron had decided to trade in his family Ford Orion sedan for a brand new BMW 325i Convertible. I didn't ask Phil if he'd got a pay rise, but I would say by the fact he was pissed off too, that he didn't get one either. A couple of part time staff joined us as well as Ron's wife and father in law to help in certain tasks as the work increased.

Back in Willen Park, we started to buy more furniture and made the house more like our home. The massive sofa was joined by a dining table and chairs that just about fitted in the small kitchen and my dad help me build a fire place covered in faux York stone brick slips and a little electric fire that a little glowing orange light that flickered and danced underneath the plastic coals, simulating a moving flame. Family from both sides came to visit us, though at times Deb did feel isolated and was beginning to feel the stress of driving up and down the motorway, driving between Milton Keynes and London because she was working at her old job, still. A job offer came from a builder's merchants in Bletchley in the Spring for Deb, that was a mighty relief to the both us as the mortgage on the house was becoming difficult to maintain as the United Kingdom was experiencing a financial meltdown, with the value of sterling in the exchange rate mechanism or ERM for short, falling to an all-time low against other currencies. Or something like that. The bottom line was that interest rates were changing nearly every week, with the letters from the building society stacking up on the kitchen worktop. One month, our rate topped out at a wopping fourteen per cent and that forty grand mortgage cost us over twelve hundred pound. We could be right in the shit if the rate increases continued for much longer. Thankfully it didn't, but what little money we had left over was used up in another one of my dumber moments as I decided to book a holiday for a belated honeymoon. At the age of twenty three, I had never been abroad before so when I saw a holiday brochure advertising the beautiful Greek island of Crete, I decided to book a flight. No hotel, no plan, just go! I popped in to the travel agent and saw this beautiful resort called Plakias in the south of the island and decided I was going to take Debbie there. She was really happy that we would be taking in some sun for a couple of weeks. I always done everything arse about face, not even booking the time of at work before I'd booked the trip but Ron was ok when I explained what the break was intended for. So we took off in April for our first foreign trip together and when we landed at Iraklion, I told Deb that I didn't book a hotel but it wasn't a problem as I had bought the holiday brochure and I would find us a place to stay. She went mental but I calmed the situation by insisting I knew what I was doing. Once inside the air conditioned Mercedes mini-cab, I opened the holiday brochure and pointed to the resort that was calling me to stay under its warm sunshine, showing the cab driver. He smiled and replied in English, "no problem". Seventy kilometres later and ninety drachma lighter, we stood in a deserted side street, looking for signs of hotels. We went into a local grocery store and asked the old gentleman who told me his name was Yorgos, if he could help. He pointed us to a whitewashed house a few metres down the narrow back road that happened to offer bed and breakfast. Debbie and I jumped at the opportunity to rest up so we approached the small house with a bit of anticipation but hope also. Entering through an open doorway, we were greeted by Helena, wife of Yorgos. It turned out to be a lovely place, our room looking out over the quiet street, with the odd donkey carrying a load, passing by, followed by an old man , shirt sleeves rolled up, cigarette hanging out of his dark tanned face and topped off with a flat cap.

Our first week was spent walking every day from the B and B to the grocery shop, getting beer and cigarettes and then spending the day in the sun on our rented sunbeds. Like I said earlier, this was my first trip abroad so I knew nothing of sun protection cream, the umbrella our only protection from the sun. Needless to say, three days later, both of us were like typical Brits abroad. Boiled lobsters! By week two, my cooked brain cells decided to buy some high factor suntan lotion but it was too late for my bloody swollen sun burnt feet. I buried them in the cool damp sand in the hope of not getting any more sun on them plus trying to ease the pain. At the end of the holiday we were basically skint, with just enough money to take a slow trip back to the airport on the local bus. Luckily for me there were two seats available on the return flight home at the front of the plane, allowing me to take my shoes off my swollen sore feet, getting some cool air circulating around my outstretched legs. Oh dear!

Chapter 20
Another Statistic

Getting back in to the groove took about thirty minutes, walking in through the rear of the shop, approaching the sales area and specifically the walk in fridge, the smell of fresh cut meat and the carpet of sawdust that covers the tiled floor reminded me what I was doing here, to work bloody hard. By the end of the first week back, my Greek holiday seemed a quickly fading memory as Saturday trading makes you switch to the part of the brain that's the auto-pilot. I would be cutting the chickens and various pork loins, belly and neck ends for spare rib chops for the window, while Phil would be cutting the stewing and frying steaks from the beef cuts hanging in the fridge. Meanwhile Ron was cutting all the beef joints to go in the main display window that we call front-runners in the meat trade, in reference to the fact they are displayed up against the glass, for the whole width of the shop window display. The price and weight tickets that were circular in shape are placed on a stainless lever pin and then placed in its accompanying roast, then lined up in straight rows like soldiers carrying a banner with its own information regarding cost, weight and price per pound, written by hand.

Going in to the second year at Marsh Farm, there was a change in attitude from Ron and his wife towards the rest of the staff as trade picked up, the business financials were getting stronger, Ron got more flashy, trading his year old 325i for another brand new BMW 635i coupe. He then bought a jet bike, followed by a speed boat. There was constant bragging about what he had and what new toy he was getting next, while me and Phil got a key ring as a gift when he returned from a family holiday to Florida. No thanks or financial bonus for building on the upward sales growth while he was away. That was enough for me to want to get away and look for another job. I called John Sergeant, another ex -Matthews shop manager turned shop owner, asking if he had vacancies. John knew me from his occasional visits to Luton when he would meet up with Ron and talk about expanding his business and show off his latest car. He was another hungry guy for all the trappings that was seen on the television, as young successful guys and girls, called YUPPIES by the media, were flaunting their champagne lifestyle in the bars and clubs of London. Built on the back of opening financial markets across the globe, traders in various commodities were getting fat bonuses and spending like there was no tomorrow and this caught the eye of news editors and programme makers, who shared the feel good factor across the various media outlets, making young guys like John aspire to want the same thing. I was no different. I dreamt of owning fancy sports cars and big houses, but that wasn't happening with my income. Sergeant offered me two hundred pounds per week after tax, considerably more than I was getting at Quality Meats and that I would start at his biggest shop that had recently opened in Weston Favell, Northamptonshire. In one year he'd opened three shops in Northampton, with a fourth opening shortly in the market town of Bicester, Oxfordshire.

It was an uncomfortable week for me when I handed in my notice to quit to Ron, especially when I told him that I was going to join up with John. I gave him my reasons for wanting to leave but he never countered the offer by increasing my salary so I took it I was subject to requirements. I drove in on my own on the final day at work using Debbie's Vauxhall Nova, said my goodbyes to everyone at the end of the working day and never looked back. My new job started at six am the following Monday, where I was greeted by Shane, the shop manager at Weston Favell who introduced me to the other staff. John was at another of his shops, sorting out staffing issues plus would be signing contracts for another two shops so I didn't see him for another week. Favell was as big as the shop in Hammersmith but even more of the latest equipment, fitted out by the best shop fitter of the time, Barlow's, who used the latest , most up to date lighting and display counters. This shop was beautiful at the front, but corners were cut by John who didn't buy enough refrigerated storage due to running out of funds, so there was times when some carcass meat had to be left wherever there was space because the only walk in fridge was full to the ceiling and the door with cuts of meat. His answer to running out of cash was to buy even more meat, getting four weeks credit and filling the display counters with cuts of steaks and chops until no more could be put in. Trade was good in the early days of this young business, John even more ruthless than Ron, Pushing staff beyond their limit of endurance as they simply couldn't cope with the pressure of twelve hour days constantly cutting so much meat. Friday was the longest day with starting at six and closing at ten pm. Staff changed often but new ones soon came, offered the biggest salary around, it was hard to say no, as I could testify. Money was flowing through the shop till and John wasn't the only one having some. Shane it turned out was a gambler and despite being the highest paid in the shop, it wasn't enough to satisfy his need to bet on horses. He openly took money out of the till and slipped off to the bookie in the shopping centre where we were situated, to have a flutter on a thoroughbred that took his fancy. One Thursday he took one hundred pounds out of the till drawer that wasn't an advance and placed bets that all lost. Another three trips to the bookies, the till now five hundred pounds short, he came back after an hour with a massive smile and a large slice of relief when his last bet came in and won him two thousand pounds. He appeared to not give a fuck as he replaced the money he used back in the till. I saw an opportunity to part him with some money as I knew he liked a sovereign ring I wore when I wasn't working. I offered it to him for three hundred quid and he agreed immediately, making me two hundred pound profit on what I paid for it. A fool and his money!

John was a fancy Dan, flash with the cash and a charmer with ladies, in and out of the shop. He was always going to night clubs with the other guys from work and I did go out with him on one occasion but it wasn't for me. He wore casual shirts that cost over a hundred pounds and thought nothing of spending hundreds on shoes and trousers and acting like a television celebrity. He certainly had a high level of arrogance that made him attractive to young women. He also spent and lost thousands of pounds on cars. He traded up his Mercedes 190E to a 350SL after the first month of me working for him. After two months of having the Mercedes convertible, he traded it in for a new Porsche 911 convertible in Red, probably after seeing one on the television, driven by a wealthy yuppie pulling away from the London Stock Exchange, making his way to their favourite wine bar. I'd been working in Northampton for four months during which in that time, he opened up his new shop in Bicester, but the turnover of the shop was much lower than what he was hoping for. He fired the manager and two of the sales assistants quit, leaving the shop with a couple of inexperienced teenagers to work in the shop. John told me to go and run the shop for him, so after blagging the tiny Suzuki company van that he had sitting idle in the service area at the rear of Weston Favell, I turned up the next morning at five thirty am where john met me to hand over the shop keys. I received his instruction on what he expected from me and the shop, while we both filled up the display counters. The shop had to take Six thousand pounds per week to break -even but was struggling to get over Four grand over the six days it was trading. We were joined by the two young guys at Seven am and within five minutes it was one member of staff when John accused the assistant of thieving , telling him to piss off. It was a crap way to deal with people and I discovered that in the short time I worked with Seargent, he had little respect for his staff because of his fucking pig-headedness. I worked at Bicester through October and November without any impact. John turned up at the shop during another quiet afternoon unannounced and embarked upon tearing me off a strip because of the shit trade. I was told to go back to Weston Favell the following morning, while Shane would be coming the other way, taking over my role. Despite my disappointment at failing to increase the trade, I was relieved to get out as I felt I was in a rut, not getting anywhere. The following morning, driving up Watling Street from my home to Northampton, I hit a patch of ice on the road as there had been a cold snap, lost control of the little van and veering up the Embankment and then doing a complete three hundred and sixty degree role before the van came to a standstill on the sloping hillside. I was shook up but escaped without injury, I immediately rang John to inform him of my lucky escape but unfortunately the van was battered up and stuck on the muddy embankment. He blew up on the phone, swearing his head off at me and it was evident he didn't give a fuck about my situation. I could understand that he would be pissed off but he never asked me if I was ok and the realisation dawned on me I wouldn't be working for this guy much longer. The recovery guy turned up about one hour later and between us , we managed to get the van back on the carriageway, gave it a quick safety check before I continued with my journey to Northampton, turning up nearly three hours late. I cracked on with filling up the display trays, Sergeant, not saying a word to me. I decided there and then this was going to be my last day and I was going to fucking double piss him off. When the shop got a little quieter, I dropped off to the cutting area in the back of the shop and boned several beef briskets and rolled them up. There was a few topsides that I cut into roll sized pieces ,bashed out the cod fat to use for basting when cooking and placed them around the corner cuts and middles, then finally tying them up, ready for sale in the shop. John left the shop about an hour before it closed. The rest of us cleared up and washed out the counters, ready for the next day. I walked out to the rear of the shop in to loading area after the close of business and made a call to John and left a message to say I was quitting with immediate effect. I opened the driver side door of the work van, wound down the window just enough to shove the key inside whilst locking the door. Deb came and picked me up to take me home and never heard from Sergeant at all. No turkey this Christmas.

Chapter 21
Tragedy

I lied when I said we got no turkey though it wasn't a big deal. I liked capons too. You could say I was impulsive in leaving two paid jobs in a few short months and did go against the advice that my dad gave me as I began my full-time career in butchery at the age of fifteen and a bit. Find a good company to progress with and work hard, stay positive through the difficult periods and do your time to work through the ranks, he said. But at twenty three I had my own thoughts, in particular about starting my own business however I didn't know where or when it was going to happen, I just had this feeling that it was possible with the knowledge I had gained by watching Ron and John run their shops and after all I had been running shops and managing staff for a couple of years, albeit for a company so how hard could it be? That maybe but I still had a mortgage to pay and Debbie couldn't cover it with her own salary so I called my dad to see if he knew of any vacancies in shops back in London. Dad had his own problems with Matthews while I was working in Luton, due to some deals he had made with suppliers who were selling meat products to him in the shops that he took charge of as a Star manager, boosting flagging sales. He didn't follow company policy by documenting purchases using consignment notes so he got fired. He was upset because he fucked up but he was back to work within a couple of weeks with a small retail butcher called Boundy, who had three shops in North and East London. Boundy was owned and ran by Marjorie and Gary, a mother and son who had picked up the business after Marjorie's husband pissed off with the contents of his bank account and a young bird. Through her pain of being shit on by her old man, this middle aged woman who had no prior experience of the meat trade, kept the business afloat, along with her only son, Gary. Back to Dad. He applied for the vacant manager's position at their shop in Station Road in Chingford, East London which was taking Three thousand pounds per week under the management of Gary. He was taken on as shop manager and within weeks the trade had doubled, down to the big meat displays plus competitive pricing. Show Big, Take Big, was his mantra. Plus he had introduced pre packed meats, tray wrapped for one pound ninety nine or three for five pounds. It was an instant success with the people of Chingford. I met Marjorie the following week and she offered me a position as a butcher in Upper Edmonton which is close to Tottenham, so I started in the second week of December nineteen eighty eight. The shop was a bloody dump, in dire need of refurbishment but there was no money to do the repairs. It still had equipment that was probably thirty years old and it even had the old cashier box from the nineteen fifties, where usually a woman would sit and take the payments from the customers after they had bought meat from the counter. This shop was also a regular target for break-ins and one had just occurred the week before I started, with the cash float being nicked out of the till. Gary came over from Chingford to run Edmonton shop with assistance from myself, Arthur, a fifty something Teddy Boy, complete with comb-back hair, DA and spiv looking pencil moustache. Gary was a good guy and made working fun again after the miserable couple of months that were now behind me. He was always cracking jokes with the customers and us working in the shop but that's not to say that he didn't graft because he did. Being the season to be jolly, we were getting all the stock in for Christmas, turkeys and cooked hams, cases of beef and capons, along with hundreds of packs of bacon rashers and sausages for the lovely fry up, the pre-cursor to the main Christmas day dinner. This wasn't the kind of shop where customers are organised and give you their list of food weeks in advance so we had to carry lots of stock as I'd already mentioned. Our regulars and the locals who used us once a year because they wanted "proper meat" and not the usual crap served by supermarkets, their words, not mine, would walk in and expect to get tasty fare for their most important dinner of the year. I can never understand this because if it was so shit at the big retail outlets, why Don't you bloody come to us the rest of the year! Because of this, Gary had to get some overnight security, to tackle any would be intruders and call the police if anyone tried to break in. Enter Phil, a retired local man who was a customer of many years at the shop and a lovely old chap to boot. The plan was that Phil would come in as we were about to close, bringing with him a dinner that could be heated up in the kitchen of the shop and watch some TV on his portable. And sniff pine disinfectant, which apparently Phil had been addicted to for a number of years. He would then be locked in all night. Thank fuck there wasn't a fire, or worse, the poor sod would overdose on the green stuff. It was funny walking in the shop to see Phil's stoned face greeting you first thing in the morning. Anyway, no break-ins or deaths occurred during my Christmas so all went well.

Back home, Deb was making our little house all festive, so it was lovely to come home to after the journey back up the grinding and often grid locked M1. We had our first Christmas at home together and our families would come up to celebrate over the holiday season. I went back to work for the day before and New Year's Eve day, closing early and driving over to Willesden to meet Deb and her family for a cracking piss up at home and then on to The Crown public house in the High Road to see in the New Year. Debbie's older sister had just given birth to a boy, so we discussed about us trying for a baby and agreed that it would be good to try though we hoped it wouldn't be twins as Deb was one and having two kids at once , shit no, we didn't want that.

Meanwhile back at work, Gary had gone to manage his other shop in Clapton, East London and his mum came to run the shop in Edmonton. She couldn't cut meat so she would sit in the telephone box-like kiosk all day, clearing the tills of cash and watching the staff, because I think she didn't trust us. This was the situation for another month, January being a shit month for business, because everyone has had their fill of meat and paying back all the debt run up on credit cards. February picked up and any butcher worth his salt would be putting on a big steak show for the ladies to buy a juicy cut of rump or sirloin on St Valentine's Day for their husbands or boyfriends. And then it turned shit for me. One afternoon, for no apparent reason, Marjorie turned funny on me, said I wasn't pulling my weight and sacked me on the spot. I was fucking gob-smacked as I thought I was doing enough to keep my job but here I was, in a situation I had never faced before. I argued back that I was doing my best but she wasn't having any of it and asked me to leave. I called my dad later that day to let him know and he seemed to side with Marjorie. Oh well, time to stop feeling sorry for myself and get job hunting. I found a post going at Jones Family Butchers in Chingford Mount, starting two weeks after getting the bullet at Boundy. It was a well-paid job, Two hundred and forty pound per week but no meat allowance. I got on well with the boss who wanted me to train his two sons who worked in the shop, on the art of cutting up dead animals. I was in the background, as in, no shop work or serving customers which for me was ok. I'd decided I was going to get my own shop and become my own boss, so the search began in North London as it made sense to work where I could get to within an hour from home. Meanwhile, the owner of Jones asked me if I knew anyone who was looking for a counter hand position, so I immediately thought of my sister, Sam, who had recently started working full time with dad in North Chingford. When I negotiated a large increase for her at my place of work, she soon joined me. We cracked on with our tasks and I was soon showing the two lads how to cut hindquarters of beef. They already had a basic knowledge of carcass cutting as their father had taught his sons how to cut lamb and pork. It was a pleasure to teach as I always get enjoyment from sharing my skills and knowledge of maximising profit and keeping waste to a minimum. Doing a costing on a side of beef, seeking out every little penny that's possible to get a good return of profit yet still being competitive so the customers keep choosing you over other businesses tells me I'm doing my job. So here we are bobbing along at the Mount which by the way I was driving there in a Datsun Cherry that I borrowed, from Milton Keynes. It had no heater and the windscreen froze up on the inside continuously on my journeys up and down the motorway during the early months of nineteen eighty nine. What a bloody nightmare! There was also the small problem that the car didn't like to start after the engine had been turned off, so wherever I stopped for longer than one hour, I had to face the car down an incline to make sure that I could bump the engine in to life when I returned.

Then deb tells me she was pregnant and we were so happy. She immediately started buying baby items and I decorated the second bedroom as a nursery as soon as she got to three months. I painted the walls in yellow, built a changing unit for the baby while Debbie was getting help from her sister Jackie and mum, Imelda. We went to Milton Keynes General Hospital for the ultra sound scans and chose an image of our beautiful baby as you do, to show the family everything was fine and through this Debbie was still working as a bought ledger clerk, though as the baby grew inside her, she struggled on and with the baby due in January, Nineteen Ninety, there was another five months to go before she would start maternity leave in December. Work continued for me unabated at Jones's through the summer of Eighty Nine though I was getting bored again and the search for a shop to purchase, continued. Through gritted teeth I stuck it out at the shop through blind faith, believing I would be my own boss as soon as I could locate the right business. Lists of shops to let came through the post at home and I travelled extensively across London.

It was the last month of the year when tragedy struck us without warning. On the 28th December, Debbie was in the fortieth and final week of pregnancy when she started to dilate so we went to the hospital expecting her to be kept in but was told by staff that there was nothing to be done until she was fully dilated and then baby would be ready to be delivered. The next few days were nerve wracking , through to the new year, when on the evening of January 2nd, Debbie felt incredible pain in her stomach and chest , we shot of too Milton Keynes general hospital in the early hours of the following morning, waiting anxiously to see a nurse. When one arrived, we explained the situation and she duly observed Debbie, turning her, this way and that. She quickly left the side ward room and we looked at each other, terrified, wondering what the hell was going on. The nurse returned with a doctor who once again checked Debbie with a stethoscope and told us that there was no heartbeat, no vital signs from our baby, that the baby was dead. We both broke down, sobbing as we held each other. The staff was trying their best to console us and then inform Debbie that she would have to go on with the pregnancy as any normal delivery, so they gave her a pessary that quickened the birth. I called our families on the phone, trying to make sense of it all, but nothing did. I sobbed, breaking down as I told Imelda that our baby had died. She had to tell me of another tragedy, that Debbie's Nan had passed away while we waited to be seen in the hospital, a few hours before and my head just reeled. I then called my mum, briefly composing myself before I started weeping and gulping in air, trying to hold myself together but hearing my mum's voice made me sob. Within a couple of hours, Debbie's family and mine arrived at the hospital, I was called to the delivery room to be with Deb and then watch through my tear filled eyes as I saw a black mop of hair, then a head and the body of my beautiful daughter arrive into the world. The midwife asked Deb if she would like to hold her, and as she did, we both broke down. The staff continued in performing their duties as we looked at our still born child, taking care of Deb as she still needed medical attention. Debbie passed our baby who we had called Shanaed, to me and as I cradled her warm body in my arms, I looked down lovingly to her and called through the tears to up above and asked why did this happen to our baby and to us. The rest of the day was a blur and I don't remember much else apart from the priest from the hospital chapel saying some prayers and the great staff helping us by providing a room that we stayed in for the next couple of days. After leaving the hospital, we travelled to Willesden to stay with Debbie's family, staying for the rest of the week, trying to work out what went wrong. I went back to work, my heart filled with pain, anger and loss, going through the motions but not wanting to be there, it was shit. After a couple of days, I decided never to return to Jones, I didn't want to explain to them my misery. While I was working, Debbie courageously organised the funeral and we picked a headstone for our baby girl, who would be buried in a children's cemetery in Milton Keynes. It was cold January morning when we had the service for Shanaed, though both our families gave us strong support and shared our pain, grief swallowed me up and my body shook as I looked down at her little white coffin in the ground, before I re-joined my wife and our families as they made their way back to the cars and the onward journey back to our house. Our futures took a different road to what should have been, both Debbie and I was scarred by this event personally, but professionally I built a steel wall in my head to block out the pain in my heart to drive myself forward.

Chapter 22
Insider Knowledge

Ok, so I am going to give you some advice regarding when it's best to shop and where, when it comes to purchasing meat. It's really common sense but try and avoid buying on a Monday morning as your butcher Will only have the cuts left over from the weekend plus they would have been delivered on the previous Friday because the big meat wholesalers including Smithfield market, work from Monday to Friday. If at all possible, leave your buying until after 12pm in which time, your friendly butcher would have got everything ready and prepared for you to choose from.

Use your senses to smell and see if the shop/kiosk/stall/supermarket counter is clean. When you approach the sales and display counter, the smells should remind you of a livestock farm without the smell of shit and the feeling of coolness as you breath through your nose, will tell you that the refrigeration is working correctly as the operating temperatures should be zero to plus four degrees Celsius for meat chillers. Look around at the shop walls, equipment and floors. Expect the odd splash of blood here and there at busy times as the priority is to serve the customers first and clean and tidy and refill the display when the queue of customers slackens off. Do the staff look clean and presentable? If they don't look after themselves, then they are not too bothered about the condition of the meat that's being sold, so steer clear and find a well-cared for shop, run by a disciplined team of butchers and their assistants. Like any skills that need to be learnt, butchery is about repetition. We perform the same tasks day in and day out. Because the display cabinets are emptied and cleaned on a daily basis at closing time, the butcher has to start early, normally around five or six in the morning depending on the size of the chilled cabinet to fill and type of meat being cut. It takes more time to cut beef and lamb than pork and chicken due to the amount of different cuts in a side of beef plus it costs a lot more to purchase so you don't want to fuck it up or you loose money. Another factor is the bigger muscles in beef and small bones in lamb take more time to cut through. Chicken is the easiest animal to cut due to the smaller number of different joints followed by the pig in the time it takes to learn how to break down in to the various sections.

KEY TO BUTCHER BACKSLANG

Back slang is used for communicating between members of staff if for example, the shop manager wanted to increase a price of a product because it was in short supply and it was necessary to make extra profit, a sales assistant could be told to increase a price in front of a customer without their knowledge. EG: *"PU THE ECRIP NET YENNUPS"*, which translates to, "up the price 10 pence". Now, you will notice not all the words are said backwards or grammatically in reverse order, but the crucial points were put across to the relevant people without the public knowing. So, here is a list though not exhaustive, to give you a taste of Butcher's back slang or *"REHCTUB KCAB GENALS"*. I will write phonetically so you can pronounce it correctly.....

NUMBERS

ONE/ENO TWO/OAT THREE/ ERT FOUR/ROAF
        FIVE/EVIF
SIX/EXIS   SEVEN/NEVIS   EIGHT/TAY NINE/EENIN
        TEN/NET

WORDS

SHIT/TISH   BREAST OR TIT/TEESAB
NO GOOD/ON DOOG   PRICK/KIRP
GOOD/DOOG   WANKER/REKNOR

GREAT OR TOP HOLE/ TEE	LAMB/BEEMAL
AITCH (T H)	PORK/KAYROP
FANNY/ YNAF	CHICKEN/DEERIB
SMELL OR SMELLY/LEMS	MONEY/YENUM
ENGLISH/TK (TOWN	POUNDS/DOONERPS
KILLED)	CHOPS/POCHIS
MEAT/TEEM	LEGS/GELS
YES/SEE	SHOULDER/REDLOCH
NO/ON	OLD/DEELO
CUNT/TINUCK	MANAGER/REJERNAM
BEEF/FEEB	BUTCHER/RECHTUB

All these words are combined to make our secret language and there are many more, some slightly different, depending on locality. If you are interested in finding out more, then I suggest you purchase *"THE SECRET LANGUAGES OF BRITAIN"* by Susie Dent.

In the follow-up book *"chop chop"*, I'll tell you about the shop we found, the violent street fights, bank robbery and kidnapping. No, this isn't a book on crime in London, just everyday life happening around me as I start life as a self-employed butcher, with my very own shop. Some great times plus tough times ahead of me. Come with me as I visit the royal residence of Clarence House for more than a cucumber sandwich and a tour, find out that running a business is more than cutting meat and making money, falling out with family and losing them too.

Review Request

Please leave a review of my book as this really helps when you share your thoughts and I would love to hear from you.

42496365R00070

Printed in Poland
by Amazon Fulfillment
Poland Sp. z o.o., Wrocław